THE BLUE RECRUIT

THE NIKOLAI DREW SERIES
BOOK 1

R. E. LIVINGSTON

Cover art and design:

Alexander P

Editor:

Sarah Grace Liu

www.threefatesediting.com

Formatter:

Liz Steinworth

www.theartofliz.com

CONTENTS

CONTENTS

My sources of inspiration,

For my Mother, Alyce M. Belknap, writer, poet, dreamer.

There are many more, if you are reading this, you know who you are, Thank You!

CHAPTER
ONE

It was pitch black, 2 a.m. on a Thursday graveyard shift, and rookie police officer Nikolai Drew, along with his training officer Corporal McNamara had stopped the dark green, four-door 1965 Impala lowrider, for a malfunctioning taillight. There were five Pacoima Trece gang members in the car, and the driver had a few outstanding warrants. Pacoima Trece was part of the Mexican Mafia or "La eMe."

As the cars rolled to a stop, McNamara walked Nikolai through his training. "Now remember kid, this hooptie is full of knuckleheads. When you get the driver's license, get a good look around the inside of the car. When you get back here, we'll run him for warrants and take it from there!" Nikolai's hand was on his side arm as he approached the driver with his flashlight firmly under his left armpit. The driver's window was down, and Nikolai could see three men in the back seat, hands on their knees. The passenger in the front seat had his hands on his knees as well.

Nikolai spoke to the driver. "Can I see your license and registration please," he asked.

The driver looked up at him as he handed the rookie his driver's license and registration and asked Nikolai, "What did I do, officer? We were just going home from a party!"

Nikolai, still poised with his right hand on his side arm, calmly and politely said, "Your left rear taillight is out. Wait here for a moment, and I'll be right back." He walked backward toward his police car, never taking his eyes off the occupants and never removing his hand from his side arm.

"What do ya got in the car, kid?" McNamara asked.

Nikolai took his handheld Motorola radio out of its case and called in a check for wants and warrants. "1-Adam-22 control, Code 10 on one." While awaiting the response, Nikolai told McNamara that there were five late-teen to early twenties Hispanics in the car, all with their hands on their knees and all sporting Pacoima Trece "13" tattoos.

The dispatcher quickly responded, "1-Adam-22, go with your Code 10."

Nikolai proceeded to read off, "Roger, California license number C0911341, last of Vasquez, first of Eziquel, no middle, last known of 465 Jackman

Street San Fernando, he is a male Hispanic, 5'7", 122, black hair, brown eyes with a DOB of 09/13/1969."

Dispatch came back with, "Roger 22, are you Code 4?"

Nikolai responded, "Not at this time, ma'am. Can you send another unit? We have five occupants."

Dispatch sent a request out for backup. "Roger, all units, be advised 1-Adam 22 is traffic on Brand Boulevard between San Fernando Road and Celis detaining five, unit to back identify?"

Before a unit could identify as the backup, dispatch came through again. "Adam-22, be advised, your subject Vasquez comes back with a Code 6 Charles for 245 P.C., again, unit to back identify!"

Nikolai knew that Code 6 Charles for 245 was a felony warrant for assault with a deadly weapon. He felt a lump in his throat, realizing that he and his partner had a potentially serious situation on their hands. If the driver was wanted and dangerous, what about the passengers?

A nearby unit responded, "1-L-27, en route, ETA two minutes," and another unit responded, "1-L-30 is enroute."

Nikolai was already walking around the driver's side of the Impala. His .45 caliber Smith & Wesson Model 645 was out of its holster, his arm by his side, gun in hand, and his flashlight was in his left hand. Before he could react, the driver of the car appeared out of the driver's door window and fired three shots toward Nikolai.

As if in the same moment, Nikolai saw the muzzle flash and felt two rounds hit him like a hammer to his chest. The impact knocked him to the ground on his back, and the back of his head struck the steel push bars of his police car. He raised his left knee, balanced his weapon, and took a shallow breath. He focused on the driver as he began to retreat into the lowrider and fired seven of the eight-round capacity at the driver of the Impala. Instinctively, he dropped the magazine from his weapon, reloaded, and held the muzzle on the vehicle, waiting to fire again if the attack continued.

No movement came from the car. Nikolai could hardly breathe, wondering just how bad he was injured, and at the same time, realizing he could hear nothing but the ringing in his ears. *Where is McNamara?* Where was the radio traffic indicating that shots had been fired? All Nikolai could think of was McNamara's Big Talk Bravado speech: *"If shots are ever fired during a traffic stop, you remove the 12-gauge Remington 870 shotgun out of the rack, and you kill every ass clown that moves in that vehicle, you hear me, kid."*

Nikolai held his weapon trained on the suspect vehicle with his right hand and with his left, removed his handheld radio from his utility belt, took a breath and calmly put out "1-Adam 22 control, shots fired, officer down, information for responding units, we are facing southbound Brand between San Fernando Road and Celis."

Dispatch responded quickly with a three-beep alert tone, "All units be advised, shots fired, Officer Down, 1-A-22 is requesting immediate backup southbound Brand between San Fernando Road and Celis, units to back identify."

Nikolai kept a watchful eye as he lay on the street praying this wasn't his final day. He remembered being in the grinder in sheriff's academy and the staff Sergeant Jimmy Stoltz looking up at him and telling him how he may be big and all, but he knew he was just a pretty boy who wanted to wear a uniform and chase women. Their job was to break a cadet down and see what they were made of, after all—then build them back up into proud officers.

Nothing more fun than running with Mister Rope for eight miles from Riverside Community College to the top of Mount Rubidoux and back, having drill instructors bark at you, singing the silliest cadence songs, and of course stopping and doing an ungodly amount of push-ups or sit-ups along the way whenever one of the cadets screwed up in one form or another—everyone had to pay for the mistake. Mister Rope was a one-and-a-half inch thick rope about fifty feet long, and they all had to hold on as they ran side by side together in formation. Nikolai recalled his nickname back then.

It was "No Sweat" because no matter how they pushed him physically, how far they ran him, he never broke a sweat. Even as he lay on the ground now, the resounding sound from a drill instructor echoed in his ear *"You're never gonna make it Drew, you know that right,"* to which his reply was always, *"Sir, no sir!"*

What seemed like hours had only been minutes as sirens from backup officers and paramedics rolled up. Sergeant "Mad Dog" Maddox walked up behind Nikolai, who was lying on the ground, and grabbed him by the collar with his right hand as he brandished a .45 with his left. "Cover us, son, I'm gonna drag ya outta this shitshow. Just relax, we got ya." Sergeant Maddox was a former United States Marine Gunnery Sergeant who served fifteen years in the Corps and did two tours in Vietnam. He was a brooding 6'4", 295-pound beast of a man and had a gruff voice that could send chills down a man's spine. Today it brought Nikolai peace knowing he was there to look out for him.

Maddox dragged Nikolai's 230-pound frame like it was a pillow all the way to the waiting paramedics behind the patrol unit. They quickly picked him up and placed him on the stretcher and wheeled him into the ambulance. In seconds, the shirt was removed, the bulletproof vest taken off, and he was assessed. Nikolai had no bullet holes in him, just bruised ribs and sternum that needed further inspection. Maddox asked Nikolai for his side arm. "Standard procedure, son. You'll get it back soon enough."

The ambulance drove off, lights and siren blaring as they checked Nikolai's vital signs and asked if he had pain anywhere. Nikolai pointed at his chest and while gritting his teeth in pain, said, "Feel like someone hit me with a tank. I can barely breathe."

The paramedic caring for him pulled the trauma plate from the bulletproof vest—a four by six-inch plate covered in Kevlar—and pointed out two protrusions and two large dents filled with lead where the suspects bullets had struck him center mass. "Whoever shot you was one hell of a good shot. Lucky you had this on. You might not be with us, had you not. How long you been on the job?"

"Six weeks," Nikolai said with a painful look on his face.

"Six weeks, and you're in the shit already," said the paramedic. "How old are you, kid?"

"Twenty-two is all." Nikolai winced.

The paramedic frowned. "Well, maybe you need to find a less hazardous line of work, son. This may be a sign."

They arrived at Holy Cross Hospital in the Emergency Port, where medical staff were standing by.

An ER doctor and a nurse assisted the paramedics who wheeled Nikolai into a private room in the ER.

"Doctor Uptugraph is my name, son. Tell me your

name and how old you are." He was an older man, heavy set and balding. He had the eyes and smile of the actor Wilford Brimley—same voice and bushy mustache as well!

Nikolai told him his name and age. The nurse was a redhead, and Nikolai glanced at her name tag as she took his left arm: Kelham. She tied a rubber tube around the area near his elbow to get a vein, slapped the area she liked a couple times, and used a cotton ball with alcohol to clean the area. She smiled at him and said with an English accent, "This may hurt a bit, hun."

Uptugraph told Nikolai that they were going to be working up an X-ray to see why he was having trouble breathing and test his bloodwork. "Any medical issues that you are aware of, son?"

"No sir," he replied.

Doctor Uptugraph placed his hand on Nikolai's shoulder, smiled, and said reassuringly, "Alright, well your blood pressure is a little high, but that's to be expected given what you have been through. I believe you are suffering from a fractured sternum or a cracked rib or two. It's nothing major, so just sit tight until we can get a picture of you, OK? Nurse Kelham will look after you. Don't piss her off—she's been known to catheterize people for being rude!"

CHAPTER
TWO

I t was now 4 a.m., and Nikolai was dozing off watching reruns of "Cannon" starring William Conrad. Nikolai laughed at himself thinking, *How appropriate!* Here he was, lying in a bed in the very same hospital where he underwent his physical, which back then he thought he would never get through successfully…

He remembered thinking it was a crapshoot because he wore contact lenses and had terrible eyesight without them, 20/600 vision to be exact, when 20/40 was the minimum any agency would accept. But then the nurse had put him in the eye exam room, enabling him to memorize the eye chart. The doctor came in and asked if he wore contacts or glasses, to which he replied that he did. The doctor instructed him to remove them and then began the test. He recited from memory, down to the 20/20 line with his left eye and down to the 20/40 line with his right eye. He put his contacts back in and went on to the color-blind test. The nurse, an attractive woman in her 50s, walked in and asked him if he had ever taken a color-blind test before. Nikolai said, "No ma'am."

She grinned. "My name is Melanie. It's a simple test. Just tell me what number stands out as we go through the pages, hun."

She opened the book and asked him to tell her what number he saw. Through the kaleidoscope of colors he read off the first three numbers, but the fourth gave him trouble. The nurse smiled at him and asked, "Are you having trouble, hun?"

When Nikolai nodded, she said, "Let me see if I can help. Pick a number between 7 and 9."

Nikolai looked at her and said, "8?"

"Very good," she said. The nurse helped him four more times in the same way.

"Am I out?" Nikolai asked.

The nurse smiled and said, "I don't know what you mean. You got them all right as far as I am concerned."

Melanie then led Nikolai to a small, padded room for his hearing test. She handed him a metal device and told him to click the button whenever he heard a beeping sound. Nikolai realized he was in trouble due to being partially deaf in his right ear. Luckily, the test began with his left ear. He heard ten beeps at three second intervals. When it came time to test the right ear, he heard five beeps and began to count three seconds from there on out hitting the button every three seconds until ten beeps should have sounded. Somehow, he managed to get through the barrage of testing.

He felt conflicted about fudging the tests. He knew they were in place for a reason. But Nikolai was 6'2" 230 pounds with a 48-inch chest, a 29-inch waist. Physically, he was a perfect specimen: he had the physique of Adonis, and he had been training in martial arts since he was five years old and began weightlifting at thirteen. In his mind, everything he'd been doing in his life was designed to get him to this point…

Nikolai stirred from the daze of his memories and looked at his watch. It was 0430, and he felt like he had been in the hospital for a month. He looked over to his left and saw Chief Belknap.

Belknap was a cop's cop, always worried about his men, and had come up in the department with Nikolai's uncle back when Parker was Chief. The look on his face was that of a worried father lurking over his son.

"How are you doing, son?" the Chief asked.

"Hey, Chief, I'm alive, just banged up a little. I am very grateful."

"Good deal, son. This is not how I wanted to see your career begin, or anyone's for that matter." The Chief continued with idle chit-chat, asking whether

Nikolai had a wife (he did not) or had notified his family (he had not), and Nikolai expressed a preference they not be notified. This would just bring heat on him about his decision to follow a path to law enforcement, a decision his mother was completely against.

Doctor Uptugraph knocked on the door then, and walked in. "Well, your labs are all splendid. You are healthy as a horse, officer. However, you do have a fractured sternum and two cracked ribs. All in all, the tape we put around you will do the job, and you will be back to 100% in three to four weeks. You are a very lucky man. You can rest up. We will release you sometime tomorrow afternoon. Get some sleep now."

Chief Belknap smiled and thanked the doctor. As the doctor left, Chief began speaking. "Look, over the next few days, there are going to be a lot of questions. I want you to remember to make sure you have a union rep and your attorney present before you talk with anyone, you understand that, son?" Just as Nikolai was going to assure him that yes, he understood, another interruption appeared at the door.

Enter Schilochian, the burly homicide detective from Los Angeles County Sheriff's Department. Schilochian pounds a bottle of Johnnie Walker Black on Nikolai's hospital bed table, pulls the cigar out of his mouth, and says in the gruffest voice one has ever heard, "Nice shootin' kid, that fucker is tagged on the toe dead! You hit him six out of seven shots all center mass, simply amazing. Don't worry about that seventh bullet—it ricocheted and hit the asshole sitting behind him. He's gonna live, but that fucker and the other three in the car all had guns as well!"

Schilochian paused as he had just realized they were not alone. "Who's this, kid, your dad?" he asked.

Nikolai winced. "Uh, no sir, that's my Chief; who are you?"

The detective developed a kind of *oh shit* look on his face and replied, "Sorry kid, Detective Sergeant Ed Schilochian, LASO. I will be investigating the officer-involved shooting for the DA's office, typical procedure ya know. Sorry to interrupt, just wanted to come in and make an introduction and congratulate you on a damn fine shooting. How long have you been on the job son?"

Nikolai looked at the Chief, who nodded that it was okay to tell him. "Six weeks, sir."

Schilochian damn near dropped the cigar out of his mouth. "Six weeks, you're shittin' me! Kid, I've seen all manner of shootings over this career, and rarely have I seen shooting like this by anyone, much less a rookie. Alright, enjoy the scotch and we'll chat later."

Nikolai looked at the Chief in shock, and if he hadn't been pale enough, he was sure he just got a few shades whiter. "The driver is dead, Chief?" he asked.

Chief Belknap stood up, curled his lip, and ran his hand over what was left of his hair and said, "Yeah, really didn't want you to hear it like this, but some guys just have no tact."

He went on. "Look, you're gonna be deskbound for a while. You will have some psychological tests and counseling to go through and a lot of interviews before this is through. You're gonna be fine. Try not to overthink things, okay?"

Nikolai was deeply concerned about his training officer, and he asked, "Chief, what happened to McNamara, did he get shot or hurt? Where is he?"

Chief Belknap shook his head and said, "Son, McNamara froze up, just froze up, but he's fine. There is a lot to talk about in time. For now, just try to get some rest, and someone will be by to talk with you later today." He started to walk out of the room and paused. He looked back at Nikolai and with all sincerity told him, "Look, I'm going to say this again, and its important, so listen up and write it down when I leave if you have to: You talk to no one unless you have your union rep and an attorney present, you understand? I mean *no one* about what happened, kid!" Nikolai shook his head in agreement, and Chief Belknap walked out the door.

The pager went off at 7 a.m. like always, Mom checkin' in for her weekly report. Nikolai was hesitant to call her back from the hospital, but figured he could improvise the conversation. He picked up the phone and dialed her number. When his mother answered the phone, he tried to speak in the most calm, like-nothing-happened kind of voice he could. His mother was damned near a clairvoyant and could sniff out trouble from anyone, especially her kids.

"Hi, Mom, how are you?"

His mother sounded worried when she responded, the tone of her voice sick with concern. "I am worried about you, honey. I saw the news about a shootout early this morning. Were you involved?"

Nikolai tried to reassure her. "It was my area, but I'm fine, Mom, nothing to worry about!"

Thankfully, the news releases for gangland shootings lacked a certain amount of detail—Nikolai was certain that his name would never be mentioned. The worry of a mother cannot be quantified, and he wasn't sure he would ever be able to calm her if she knew.

She finished off with, "Well, I am glad you weren't in that horrible mess. Love you. Call me later, okay?"

Nikolai was jovial and responded with a lighthearted, "Sure Mom, once I get caught up, I'll head your way for a visit. I love you to pieces."

"Okay, honey, will do, call me later. Love you too." His mother hung up the phone.

Nikolai then called his home number hoping to get ahold of his sister. The answering machine picked up, so Nikolai left a message that he was going to be in Los Angeles for a few days working, but would be in touch again later or to page him if she needed anything.

Unbeknownst to Nikolai, Nurse Kelham was standing at the doorway listening to his conversation. "Isn't that sweet," she said with her heavy British accent as she walked in.

Nikolai blushed.

"Nothing to be ashamed of love, nice to see a man in uniform still takes the time to call his mum and tell her he loves her, quite endearing really."

Nikolai grinned sarcastically, feeling like he was in high school being called out as a momma's boy. Nurse Kelham took his pulse and checked his IV to make sure he was doing well.

"Nurse, why do I have an IV if I didn't lose any blood?" he asked.

"Well, first of all, I'm Melanie and we give IV solutions to people in shock, which you were in when you got here, love. Did you manage to get any sleep?"

He thought for a moment. "Yes, finally a little, till my pager went off."

"That's good. I'll be back to check on you later. Try to get some more rest," she said. He was just about to nod off when he realized that Nurse Kelham was the same nurse that had tested him during the hiring process. He also suddenly realized he needed to use the bathroom. The pain in his chest rattled Nikolai to the bone, but he managed to reach over and press the call button to ask for help, then sat back in his hospital bed, pondering whether or not Nurse Kelham recognized him or not.

Nurse Kelham came in and said laughing "Missed me already, did ya!" She helped him up and reminded him to walk the IV pole with him and carefully. He managed to get to the restroom and return with more ease than expected. The saying "A body in motion tends to stay in motion" made all the sense to him, particularly now.

CHAPTER
THREE

When Nikolai next awoke, there were two men by his bedside. They introduced themselves as Corporal Picarone, the union representative from the police department assigned to watch over him, and Paul Payne, who would be acting as his attorney and was a former battlefield Marine.

"What can I do for you, gentlemen?" Nikolai asked.

Picarone grinned and said, "Well, we're here to take your badge and gun!"

When Nikolai turned sheet-white, Picarone laughed. "Relax, man, we're here to chat about the incident and make sure you are ready for when you give your statement to the detectives."

Both men were sitting bedside, and Payne asked him to recall everything that happened.

Nikolai began, "It's about 0100 hours, and I see this green, lowered Chevy Impala traveling at sixty plus miles per hour through the twenty-five zone in the San Fernando Mall with a broken taillight. It was dark as hell, and the old streetlights barely provided any light at all. McNamara looked at me with an indignant stare. 'Well, are you waiting for an engraved invitation?' he said. I accelerated, turned on the red and blues, and the Impala turned onto South Brand from San Fernando Rd., slowly pulling to the curb. McNamara asked me where we were. I told him that we were headed southbound on South Brand from San Fernando Road, sir. So I put out the stop and the license place, YXC023 I think."

Nikolai proceeded to tell Picarone and Payne the events that had led him here, adding, "There was no movement or talking from McNamara. From what I could tell, he had not put out a help call, and there were no blasts from a shotgun killing everyone in the car like he told me to do if he ever got shot in a gunfight! Anyway, the rest is as you know, I called for backup, and after what felt like an eternity, Sergeant Maddox grabbed me by the collar and dragged me out of the line of fire. That's all I got, fellas."

Picarone interjected, "Well, that is pretty much the statement of the passengers of the car and of McNamara. Mac just choked, froze, and did nothing. When backup arrived, he was catatonic. The man was in shock, and we finally got him talking this morning. I listened to the tape of your backup request. It's eerie, man. You were calm and detailed. Sergeant Maddox told me that he honestly thought you were reporting and thought McNamara was the one who got shot.

"You handled this particularly well," Attorney Payne said. "Your shots into the vehicle were inside a six-inch radius, and six out of the seven shots hit the driver center mass. The only thing that stopped the seventh round was the bullet that hit the frame of the car. It bounced off and struck the passenger sitting directly behind the driver. Every asshole in this car was carrying and there were a ton of weapons and meth in the trunk."

"Tell me, Paul," Nikolai asked. "What was this guy's rap sheet like?"

Attorney Payne responded, "Well, he's a real piece of work, forty-three years old, lifelong MS-13 gang member. He'd done prison stints, one for five years at Corcoran for assault on a police officer and possession of a kilo of methamphetamine. The other was a seven-year jolt at Lompoc for armed robbery and attempted murder—shot the clerk, who lived. I spoke with Detective Sergeant Schilochian from the LA Sheriff's Department, and he is already convinced it's a clean shoot. He just wants to hear your side of the story so he can get the report out. I will set something up in a few days, once you feel like it."

Nikolai nodded. "I am ready any time. Just let me know, Paul."

Picarone cautioned, "Do me a favor, Nikolai, don't speak to anyone about this thing, at all. The less you say right now the better. Once the shooting review board gets done with this, you can breathe. Just don't talk to anyone, and especially don't talk to anyone without us present."

Nikolai nodded again, understanding, and asked, "What happens next?"

Picarone put his hand on Nikolai's shoulder. "Well, you'll be flying a desk until you're cleared for duty. You'll have an appointment with the department psychologist. She will chat with you and probably administer the MMPI or some other written psychological test or maybe two, no different than the ones you took to get hired. If you pass psych, you will be cleared to return to training. Also, so you're aware, there could be a civil suit for wrongful death that comes out of this. The outcome of the shooting investigation will likely squash that, but one never knows."

The worry on Nikolai's face was obvious. "Could I get fired over this or lose everything in a civil suit? I mean, I am just a rookie, and I feel like I am just a liability?"

Payne stood up, looked at him, shook his hand and explained, "You're a hero, kid. You took a beating and handled the incident leaving no liability on the department. I can tell you, after speaking with the Chief, he is extremely proud of you and the way you are handling it. You have a good head on your shoulders and a good heart. Don't sit around worrying about things out of your control." Handing Nikolai his card, Payne closed by saying, "Page me anytime. I will get right back to you."

Picarone started to follow Payne out and Nikolai asked, "Do you have any tips about the psych test?"

Picarone stopped, sat back down, and asked him, "Well, you're going to get quizzed on how you feel about killing a man. How do you feel about that, Nikolai? You are going to need to think about how you're going to answer this so you don't sound like you're conflicted or holding something back. I am like your attorney, you don't have to hold back with me, and I am sure as hell not recording this. Just tell me how you're feeling."

He pondered for a moment. "Well, I feel like I defended myself, and at the end of it, a man died. I don't feel good about it, but I don't feel bad either."

Picarone grinned. "You are bound to go through some different emotions going forward, everyone acts differently. You have family members that were cops, right? You may want to chat with them, I am sure they will have some fascinating insight about what you are going to go through in the coming weeks."

CHAPTER
FOUR

Thinking back to the academy, Nikolai remembered his interview after interview, repeated background paperwork submission, and how, despite being the top cadet academically and physically, he'd become frustrated with making the top three or better on a list and still being told he was on a waiting list. September of 1986, two guys from LAPD showed up early in the morning at the Riverside Sheriff's Academy: Sergeant Bill Maddox and Detective Bob Glass. They were off in the distance just scouting to see who was who. They would be recruiting over the next few days and liked the Riverside Sheriff's Academy because it had a lot of candidates who were motivated and put themselves through as college students.

On this day, the class leader, William Satmary, was not his punctual self, and everyone was just milling about. Nikolai decided to step up and get everyone in formation as no one else seemed to particularly care. The penalty for not being in formation and ready when the academy tack staff arrived was push-ups till they died, or another long winded run to the top of Mount Rubidoux, or Mount Mother Fucker as they loved to call it, which was eight miles from Riverside Community College and back.

Then that *oh shit* moment hit—Jimmy Stoltz, the Sergeant from Riverside Sheriff and the Academy Continuity Officer, walked up behind Nikolai and whispered in his ear, "What the fuck are you doing up here, Drew, and where in God's name is Satmary?"

Nikolai snapped to attention and said, "Sir, I have no idea, sir. I am just getting everyone ready for morning drill, sir."

Stoltz whispered again, "Well fall in, you idiot, before I snap my size twelve off in your ass."

Meanwhile, Cadet Satmary was running as fast as he could from the parking lot and arrived out of breath, stood before Stoltz at attention, and saluted, apologizing for being late. Stoltz accepted his apology and then made every one of them drop and give fifty push-ups as punishment for Satmary's tardiness.

Over the next three days, Sergeant Maddox and Detective Glass observed everything from studies and lectures to shooting range conduct to practical scenarios where cadets pretended to roll into shooting scenarios, etc. Ultimately, they asked about two cadets, Nikolai Drew and Hector Garcia, to see how they were favored academically and physically and how they were looked upon by staff and their fellow cadets. Nikolai was at the top of the list for the academy, rated number one physically and academically. As for Garcia, Nikolai was amazed that they selected the arrogant narcissist, causing him to ponder what they thought of him.

Sergeant Maddox gave Stoltz two application packages for employment, one for Drew and Garcia, which Stoltz provided to the cadets at the end of that day. Luckily, this was a Thursday, which gave them ample time to get in touch before the end of the week.

Friday morning came around and after physical training and getting a quick shower, Nikolai called the number on one of the business cards included with the application, asking for Detective Glass. The secretary for the Detective Division answered and transferred the call to Glass. Nikolai introduced himself, and Glass confirmed that they had a few slots to fill and said that they didn't play by the rules of affirmative action like the Inland Empire and Orange County, explaining they are already well integrated and just need quality bodies to fill the positions.

"I am glad you called this morning, shows you are motivated," Detective Glass said. "We have a panel set to interview you this Sunday at ten a.m. We set this up for you on Sunday because we know you have a lot going on with the academy and want to accommodate you. You will need to provide that full background package you received that day as well as the application we left for you. If you pass the three-person interview, you will go right in for your Chief's interview. We are waiving the physical training test because you're number one in your academy physically and we personally witnessed you perform all of the tests. We were quite impressed. Now, I want to also set you up for a ride along tomorrow during swing shift. That is from three p.m. to eleven p.m., and it will get you an idea of what you are up against and see if you like the department and some of the team. Can you make that happen?"

Nikolai had merely been listening and when asked, could hardly maintain his excitement. He responded, "Absolutely, sir, I will be there,"

Glass said, "That's great. It's a bit of a drive, so prepare for about two hours to get here. I'd also recommend you stay at a hotel as well. The drive back and forth can be a killer."

"I will be there with bells on, sir. See you tomorrow."

CHAPTER
FIVE

All day, Nikolai had a spring in his step. He knew he was going to be up late filling out paperwork—the background and application forms were about forty-eight pages, but he had copies of the ones already submitted prior, and it would be easy just transferring the information over. He ended the day at the academy at 4:30 p.m., went home, and got everything filled out. The next morning Nikolai got up, showered, shaved, packed a bag, prepared a suit and put on slacks and a polo shirt to head in for his ride along. He arrived in the area early and found a hotel room close by the police station. He went up, dropped off his bag, and freshened up before heading to the police station to check in.

I lobby of the worn-down station carried a dank, musty smell. It was either vomit, the linoleum floor, the old vinyl covered chairs in the lobby or a combination of all the above. He approached the bulletproof glass and rang the assistance bell. The bright white walls and the fluorescent lights reminded him of an old *Adam-12* scene. A female in uniform came to the glass. "Can I help you?" she asked.

Nikolai replied, "Yes ma'am, I am here for a ride along. Detective Glass told me to give you his name."

The woman handed Nikolai a clipboard and told him to fill out the form, sign it, and bring it back up with his driver's license when he had it completed. After a few minutes, Nikolai returned to the glass and slid the clipboard and his license to the uniform-clad woman who took it, smiled and said, "Give me a few and I'll be right with you." Moments later, she returned at the side door and told Nikolai to come with her.

They walked down the hallway littered with old photos of law men from years past and entered the squad room where they conducted roll call. There was a chalkboard up front, six long tables, old wood chairs, and a podium, reminiscent of a science lab from Nikolai's high school days, which weren't really all that long ago. The room stank like a transient who hadn't showered for a year. She sat him up front and told Nikolai to hang out and that the Sergeant and the gang would be out shortly.

At 1430 hours, in walks a tall well-built man with sergeant stripes on his sleeves. "You must be

Nikolai," the man said with a smile. He stuck out his hand and introduced himself. "I am Sergeant Brodie, nice to meet you."

Nikolai greeted him in return, then Brodie said, "I have a ride along set up for you with one of our training officers. He's a character, but once he warms up to you, he is a good guy. His name is Mike Fricassi."

The Sergeant continued. "Anyway, this is really just an opportunity for you to see if you like the place and make sure you know what you are getting yourself into. I hear you are quite the student at the academy, first in class physically and academically, yes?"

Nikolai was a little embarrassed, but he answered yes with humility.

"Do you have family on the job?" the Sergeant asked.

Nikolai smiled. "Yes sir, I will be a sixth-generation law man if I make the process. How about you?"

Brodie grinned. "No, all my family are teachers, construction workers, and shit like that. I am the black sheep of the family and first to become a cop, ever!" Nikolai looked at him puzzled, and Brodie went on. "Yeah, been a cop for eighteen years and have loved every minute of it! Anyway, I have to get ready for roll call. The gang will be in shortly. There's coffee and water in the break room across the hall. Make yourself at home."

Police officers began entering the room, twelve of them altogether, and they scattered throughout the room, chatting and milling about, setting their posse boxes, flashlights, and riot batons on the tables. It sounded like a bowling alley as all of them seemed to send them down on the tables in unison. Fricassi walked into the room. He was a bit overweight, with grayish blonde hair, carrying his posse box and a cup of coffee. He immediately eyed Nikolai and made his way to the front table and sat down. He took a sip of his coffee and held out his hand. "Fricassi, what's your name?"

Nikolai gripped the officer's hand. "Drew, Nikolai Drew, good to meet you."

Fricassi eyed him up and down. "Yeah man, you too, let's get through this roll call thing, and we can get to the business of getting' to the field."

Brodie barked at the unruly mob of law men. "Listen up, all was pretty quiet today. We have three calls holding, which will be assigned as soon as you clear briefing. Detective Bedo will be coming in shortly to give you the scoop on a homicide and suspect description from earlier today."

As they waited for the detective, Sergeant Brodie read off unit assignments to the patrolmen:

"3-L-20 (K-9 Floater) Fabriovetti
3-L-22 (Pacoima) Kazminski
3-L-23 (Sylmar) Big George
3-A-25 (The Rock) Vasquez and Baker
3-A-26 (Arleta) Burns and Wardlow
3-L-27 (Pacoima) Hanrahan
3-L-66 (Rover) Martinez
K-9-3 (Rover as usual) Fabriovetti."

"Fricassi, you will work as CRASH 1 tonight. Find the kid some fun and try not to get him killed."

Bedo walked in and began handing out flyers to everyone. "Okay, gang, especially CRASH, keep an eye out for this cat. We have eyewitnesses giving a positive ID as a shooter near Hansen Dam killing two black males with a semi auto handgun at close range. His name is Alex Garcia aka 'Jaws' and is with Mara Salvatrucha 'MS-13.' His descriptors are on the sheet I handed out, the BOLO. He is armed and extremely dangerous. This guy has MS-13 across the front of his entire neck, folks, and a crazy clown tattoo face covering the entire back of his shaved head. This guy is full blown nuts, so watch your six if you come across him."

Brodie dismissed the squad, and they all walked out into the hallway. Some of the officers introduced themselves to the would-be rookie, but most didn't give Nikolai the time of day. Bedo approached Fricassi and Nikolai and said, "Watch your ass tonight. This guy is on foot, and his rap sheet is more violent and longer than my Johnson. I'm gonna be creepin' around tonight, so if you need me, radio me."

Fricassi and Nikolai made their way to the plain wrapped Caprice in the back of the station, and Fricassi showed Nikolai how to do a vehicle inspection, noting the flares, emergency kit, and blankets in the trunk as he threw his war bag in the back. Fricassi asked Nikolai if he had shotgun experience with loading and so forth, and Nikolai said he did. Fricassi handed him the Remington 870 pump-action shotgun and told him to load it up.

"It takes six rounds in the magazine, but make sure you don't rack one in the chamber, then slide it into the rack in the unit." Nikolai made short work of the assignment and watched as the overweight man with two stripes on his sleeve checked the rest of the unit.

Fricassi looked over at Nikolai. "Okay, kid, welcome to the big leagues. We're working a gang detail tonight—that's what CRASH is, Community Resources Against Street Hoodlums—and we're on the hunt for assholes and specifically this assclown Jaws. So, as we drive around keep your eyes open. When we stop pedestrians or cars in traffic stops, I want you to get out of the car and act like you're a detective. Just look like you mean business, but don't say anything. If shit goes sideways, I want you to back me up and help me detain whoever we are dealing with, got it? If I go down, there is a 5 shot .38 in my left rear pocket, and of course, you know how to operate the shotgun rack, yes?"

Nikolai responded, "You go it, sir, back you up and shut the hell up."

Fricassi nodded. "Alright, let's go get dirty," he said, and they entered the unmarked unit.

The second they were up and running, Fricassi took a backup call. Big George, Unit 3-L-23, had gone Code 6 on four pedestrians at Dronfield and Hubbard (meaning he was jacking up four dirt bags) and was requesting an additional unit. Fricassi put it out over the police radio: "Crash-1 enroute to back 23, two-minute ETA."

Immediately Fabriovetti came over the air: "3-L-20, En Route to back 23 as well."

Fricassi looked over at Nikolai and said, "Well, that will shake things up a bit. Gangsters hate the dog!"

Nikolai grinned.

Fricassi told Nikolai, "Pick up the mic and tell dispatch Crash 1 is out with 23 at Dronfield and Hubbard." Nikolai took the mic and put it out like he had done it all his life.

As they pulled up, Fricassi told Nikolai to stand out of the car, but to stay by the passenger door, which he did, with his Maglite under his armpit.

Big George already had the four gangbangers sitting on the curb, feet out in front, crossed with their hands on their knees. He had begun the arduous task of patting them each down for weapons and or drugs, and then they would fill out a field interview card. Once all done, he'd run them for wants and warrants. Nikolai watched intently as Big George patted down each of the pedestrians one by one, then put them back at the curb, all the while Fricassi stood ominously in the back watching closely. When the patting down was complete, and there were no weapons found and no drugs, Big George began getting their ID cards and filling out field interview cards. Fricassi took the cards and walked over to Nikolai and radioed in to dispatch. "Crash-1, clear to Code 10 four subjects." Dispatch replied "Roger Crash-1, go with the first subject."

Fricassi rattled off the information like a soldier, until all four were called in, leaving a pause on each one to make sure that radio traffic was left open in case another officer had an urgent call to put in.

One of the four detainees ended up having a warrant for weapons charges, a good felony sting. They let the other three go, and Big George cuffed and transported the guy, Enriquez, into the station for booking.

Fricassi and Nikolai got back in their unit, and Fricassi put out over the air "Crash-1 10-8," meaning they were in service again. Three hours into the shift, Nikolai pointed out an expired registration and burned-out driver side taillight on a lowered '66

Chevy El Camino. Fricassi looked at it and noted there was a Hispanic gangbanger in the car.

Fricassi turned the unit around and called in the plate, and dispatch responded, "Crash-1, no want or warrant, vehicle comes back expired registration, June of 1985 to Hugo Ochoa at 465 Jackman Street." Fricassi notified dispatch that they were stopping the vehicle. "Crash-1 control, be advised we are on a traffic stop on that vehicle S/B Sepulveda just North of Van Nuys." Dispatch parroted the information.

Nikolai hit the overhead red light which is mounted stealthily in front of the car's windshield mounted rear view mirror and hit the siren briefly to get the driver's attention. The '66 El Camino slowed to a stop in front of them at the curb.

Fricassi told Nikolai as they rolled to a stop, "Remember, get out, put the spotlight on the passenger side of the car, and watch my back." Fricassi got out and immediately approached the driver's side door of the El Camino. As he approached, he noticed a damn crazy clown face on the back of the driver's head.

Calmly he approached and contacted the driver, who was alone in the car, and told him to keep his hands on the steering wheel. He asked for his license and registration.

The driver looked up at Fricassi, hands on the steering wheel. "May I ask why you stopped me, officer?"

Fricassi stated, "Sure, your driver rear taillight is out, and your registration is expired. May I see your license and registration now please?" Fricassi could see clearly this guy was Jaws as he had the MS-13 tattoo across the front of his entire neck.

Jaws looked up at Fricassi and handed him his license. Jaws sarcastically said, "Look, Ese, I borrowed this car from my cousin, I have no idea where the registration is, and honestly, I had no idea it was expired."

Fricassi smiled. "Not to worry, I'll be right back and will get you on your way."

As he walked back to the car, keeping an eye on the driver, he looked down and realized the license was in fact the suspect named in the shooting, "Alex Garcia."

Fricassi called in to dispatch, "Crash-1 control, we are traffic on wanted subject Alex Garcia, requesting an additional unit at our location, suspect is armed and dangerous." Dispatch put out the request, and Bedo responded first, "13-David, en route, seven-minute ETA." Two others cued up as well.

Nikolai looked at Fricassi. "That's our guy, right?"

Fricassi looked excited. "Shit, yes, kid, so hold on, backup is on the way."

Just then, they heard the car turn over—Jaws was attempting to start it up! Fricassi and Nikolai moved like they were returning to the unit, but the El Camino wouldn't start. Jaws emerged from the driver's door of the El Camino, turning back toward the police car. Fricassi engaged the man, and the fight was on. Jaws hit Fricassi in the mouth, and Fricassi hit him back, right across the nose then kicked him in the groin with his right knee, and that was all she wrote.

Fricassi's back went out, and he dropped to the ground in pain, now lying on his side in the middle of the street, incapacitated. Nikolai came up behind Jaws while Fricassi held on with all he had. Nikolai grabbed his right hand, twisted it around Jaws's back, and applied a wrist restraint as he worked Jaws's arm behind him. Nikolai pressed his stomach into the elbow of the man and applied pressure enough to get Jaws screaming, "Back off, mother fucker, you're gonna break my fuckin wrist!"

Nikolai commanded, "Put your left hand on top of your head." There was no cooperation so Nikolai slammed Jaws's face into the side of the El Camino and said quietly with authority as he applied pressure, "I said put your fucking hand on your head or I will snap this hand clean off your wrist!"

Jaws whimpered. "Alright man, fuck, back off!"

Jaws raised his left hand to the top of his head, and Nikolai looked down at Fricassi and told him to hand him his cuffs. Fricassi struggling, managed to reach the cuffs and hand them up to Nikolai. He slapped the one cuff on the left wrist, which was still on Jaws's head, then swung the arm behind the man

R. E. LIVINGSTON

and attached the other cuff to his wrist. Nikolai leaned Jaws over the hood of the crash unit, spread his legs, and patted him down like he was trained in the academy. No weapons, but there were some baggies he pulled out that looked like a powdery substance consistent with that of cocaine. Nikolai put Jaws in the car, locked the doors, and went back to aid Fricassi. He moved him out of the lane of traffic just as Detective Bedo pulled up. Unit 20, Fabriovetti also arrived. Bedo put out a request for an ambulance noting that an officer was down, but that the situation was under control.

Bedo was getting the story from Fricassi and Nikolai as Sgt. Brodie arrived. Bedo and Nikolai were kneeling on the ground, and Fabriovetti had removed the suspect and was patting him down again, just to make sure nothing got missed while his dog "Dickey" sat patiently watching. You could see Dickey was hoping the suspect would breathe wrong. Dickey was a land shark after all, and loved putting the bite to bad guys!

Meanwhile, Fricassi was telling Bedo and Sergeant Brodie what happened and noting that had it not been for Nikolai moving quickly and instinctively, this could have ended very badly.

Nikolai stood off to the side, pondering the outcome of this clusterfuck, hoping he didn't just flush his chances of getting hired with this department right down the toilet.

The ambulance arrived, loaded Fricassi onto a stretcher, and transported him to Holy Cross Hospital, a contract hospital for the city, less than five miles away.

Sgt. Brodie looked at everyone and asked Bedo to transport the dirtbag "Jaws" to the station. Bedo agreed, and Brodie looked at Nikolai. "Kid, follow us back to the station in the detective unit, will ya. Just pull it in on the patrol side and park it there."

Nikolai acknowledged the Sergeant, got in the car, and followed them to the station. They walked the dirtbag into the sally port, then into booking, and handed him over to the booking officer for processing. Bedo and Sgt. Brodie walked Nikolai into the hallway out of the jail and patted Nikolai on the back. Sgt. Brodie was laughing like a kid watching a comedy act. "Well, that was pretty damn amazing, kid! You just got in the fight of your life, saved one of the boys and managed to even detain the dirtbag! Not a bad day's work for a green pea! Well, your ride along is over. Head out and get some rest before your interview tomorrow morning. It's nearly 2300 hours, and you are gonna need to be at your best tomorrow!"

Nikolai went back to his hotel room and reviewed his paperwork, including all the transcripts they wanted, driver's license copy, and social security card. It was all there ready to be turned in. He turned on the radio in the room and nodded off to sleep.

Nikolai left the hotel at 7:30 A.M. so he could

drive around, get a feel for the area, and even have a light breakfast. He hopped in his part primer gray, part blue '69 Chevy El Camino and headed out to Los Angeles. The El Camino might have looked rough, but the 350 horse and the turbo 350 trans and 12 bolt rear end were solid. Plus, the air conditioning worked. He arrived in the valley at 9:15, drove around for a bit, and stopped at a place called Pancake Heaven for some breakfast. He had coffee, three eggs over easy with bacon, hash browns, and an English muffin, burnt. While sitting there, two police units pulled in, and three officers walked in and sat down. He watched as they ordered and joked around a bit, and he had a feeling come over him like he was finally going to become what he dreamed of: a cop, just like his dad before him, his uncles, and his dad's dad before him.

Nikolai made the drive ten minutes away to Foothill Station where the interview would be conducted, just down the street from the Van Nuys Airport off Osborne Street in Pacoima, a place littered with gang graffiti and interesting characters walking about the streets. At the desk, he asked the officer to please page Detective Glass. A few moments later Glass came out front and shook Nikolai's hand with a smile. "Nice to see you, son."

Nikolai smiled. "I'm a bit early, sir, just wanted to make sure I wasn't late."

Glass guided him into the station. "That's great.

Do you have your paperwork for me?" Nikolai handed him the envelope, and Glass asked, "Did you bring a suit for the interview?"

"Oh, yes sir, I just didn't want to get it wrinkled on the way, it's in my car."

"Smart move son," Glass said. Grab it and meet me back here in a few minutes, I'm gonna turn this paperwork over to the panel who's interviewing you and I will be right out. Since you are early, I can take you on a tour of the facility before your interview." They parted company, and Nikolai retrieved his suit from his El Camino and waited for Glass in the lobby.

Glass walked out from the secured area and brought Nikolai into the squad locker room to change. Nikolai got changed into his suit, and minutes later, Glass returned to escort the young recruit around the station. He got to see dispatch, the locker room, the shooting range, and finally the Detective Bureau. Glass asked Nikolai to have a seat and await an escort to the interview.

Nikolai was in awe of the wanted boards, the desks in disarray, and the musty smell. It reminded him of his father's old precinct house in New York: old, tarnished, but always humming from the business that was being conducted 24/7.

Glass proudly showed off his desk. "This is where the magic happens, kid. I am currently working on forty cases. Some are cold, but a lot of follow up is taking place with search warrants and arrests on the way. Last month, I closed a triple homicide that took place over six months. A banker murdered three customers all dealing with precious gems out of their homes! He tied them up, bound and gagged them, and after he robbed them, slit their throats and let them bleed to death. You know how I caught them?"

Nikolai was intrigued. "You caught him trying to sell off the gems?"

Glass immediately said, "I caught him, yeah, trying to sell off the gems. It was a lot of fishing and just good luck really, but we got him and managed to get the murder weapon as well as the confession." He started to elaborate, and the door opened.

Sgt. Maddox, the big burly cop who had accompanied Glass at the Riverside Sheriff's Academy stepped into the detective's office. "Send him in, Bob," he said with a gruff deep voice.

Nikolai entered the room. The dark blue suit, white shirt, red tie, and highly polished shoes just topped the presentation. It was his muscular 6'2" frame with a flat-top haircut and mustache that brought together the total package. The three men introduced themselves, Lieutenant Jim Smith, Sergeant Bill Maddox, and Corporal Bob Jacobs.

The lieutenant said, "We have a barrage of questions for you, Nikolai. Just breathe and don't overthink things."

Lieutenant Smith started off with the first question. "You are working patrol and enter a store with your partner. You observe him pick up a pack of gum and put it in his pocket, making no attempt to pay the cashier. What do you do? Do you A.) Have a chat with him and make him put it back or pay for it B.) Tell your patrol Sergeant what you witnessed or C.) Ignore it like it never happened."

Nikolai remained quiet for a moment, then stated, "Sir, I would get in the station and report it to my Sergeant. We are charged with the public trust, and frankly, if we don't hold one another accountable, it's just a matter of time before the entire system falls apart."

Sergeant Maddox speaks up. "Alright, rookie, you make a traffic stop on a lone female at night for speeding. You pull her over and ask for her license, registration, and proof of insurance. She is obviously intoxicated and tells you that she will provide you with any kind of sexual favor you desire if you just let her go. What do you do? Do you go about your investigation and eventually arrest her for DUI, or do you take her around the corner and take her up on her proposition, then let her go?"

Nikolai responds again quickly, "I will continue my investigation, and if she is driving under the influence, she will be arrested. If not, the very least will be a speeding ticket, sir."

Corporal Jacobs finished up with one last question. "Nikolai, why do you want to be a cop?"

Nikolai paused for a moment and after wrapping

his head around what he had gone over in his head, every single time he had interviewed before. He said simply, "Sir, there is a strong need for dedicated people in law enforcement today, not people who just want a job or want to wear a badge because they want to wield power over others, but those who want to legitimately serve and fill a void. I am a sixth-generation law man, and honestly, this is all I have ever wanted to be."

The lieutenant asked, "One last question, Nikolai. If you are selected, what do you want to do with a career in this department?"

Nikolai looked back and forth at all three of the men before him and said confidently, "I want to educate myself and I want to do every job there is within the department and see where that leads me. Hopefully I will grow into this and maybe even work my way up to Chief of Police one day, sir."

Lieutenant Smith stood and shook Nikolai's hand, as did the other two men. They told Nikolai to have a seat in the hallway and await further instructions.

Nikolai felt good, but he had felt that way before. He waited nearly thirty minutes, and Glass walked up and took him for a walk. Glass told him that they were highly impressed with the answers given as well as the way he dressed and overall appearance. He said, "The Chief is on his way in to see you, and once that is done, we will chat again. Have a seat in the lobby, and I will come get you when he is ready for you."

While waiting in the lobby, a sharply dressed officer walked in, wearing two stripes below his department patch which Nikolai knew signified a corporal rank. He was about 5'9", stocky, and built like a bodybuilder crossed with a wrestler. The name on his plate adjacent to his badge was Picarone. Sitting next to Nikolai, he held out his hand and introduced himself. "I'm Lou Picarone, nice to meet you, I'm a Field Training Officer. Just wanted to say what a great job I heard you did during your ride along!"

Nikolai smiled and thanked him.

"Have you been through the oral interviews yet?"

Nikolai replied, "I've been through the panel interview and am now waiting for the Chief to come in."

Picarone asked him, "Well, how do you think you did?"

Nikolai replied with a bit of confidence, "I answered the questions from the heart and told them what I would do if I was selected for hire. I really think I couldn't do any better, sir."

Picarone stood up, shook his hand again and said, "Well, I hope you make it. You seem like a solid kid, and I think you'd make a great addition to the department. Besides, you're not an overconfident assclown with an ego bigger than Brooklyn, if you know what I mean! Little hint, if the Chief asks you if you live out of the area and would you relocate, be sure to tell him yes, whether you would or not. That's a biggie to him." Picarone walked off, looked back with a thumbs-up and said, "Break a leg, rookie."

Glass walked back into the lobby. "You ready, kid? The Chief is ready for you."

Nikolai was nervous and confident and stressed all at the same time. They were buzzed into the main corridor and made their way down the long, narrow dimly lit hall that led to the Chief's office. To Nikolai, it felt like an hour-long walk, when in reality it was less than two minutes.

Glass walked in first and said, "The candidate is here. You ready for him, Chief?"

Nikolai heard the Chief jovially reply, "You bet, send him in."

As Nikolai walked into the room, Chief Daryl Belknap was leaning against the outside edge of his desk. He was lean, 5'10", and his uniform was impeccable. There were four stars on each collar, medals that covered his right breast, and so many hash marks that signified years of service that one could not possibly count without staring. Chief Belknap leaned forward, sticking his hand out, and as they shook hands he introduced himself. "Chief Belknap, son. You're Nikolai Drew, yes?"

Nikolai stood over the Chief by several inches and

was massive in stature, but it didn't feel that way. "Yes sir, it's an honor to meet you."

There was a couch and two chairs in front of the Chief's desk, and as the Chief took a seat on the couch, he told Nikolai to have a seat. Belknap leaned forward with his elbows on his knees and looked at Nikolai intently. "You're Jack Smith's nephew, aren't you?"

"Yes sir, I am, he has great stories about the two of you growing up together through the academy and on the department," Nikolai said.

Belknap laughed. "Well, Jack's a liar! Tell me what makes you tick, Nikolai., Why do you want to be a cop?"

Nikolai pondered for a moment and said, "Chief, I feel there is a strong need for dedicated people in law enforcement, not just men or women who want to wear a badge and enforce laws, but honestly, to serve and honor the philosophy of enforcing the spirit of the law versus the letter of the law. I'm a sixth-generation law man and honestly, this career is all I have ever wanted."

Belknap smiled. "Did you write that, or did you just spit it out impromptu?"

Nikolai paused for a moment before he responded, "It's similar to what I said in the interview, but I just spoke from the heart, Chief."

Belknap laughed a bit. "Well, son, that is honestly

the best damn answer any candidate has ever given, at least to me that is. Do you live in Los Angeles?"

Nikolai responded, "No sir, I don't. I live in Riverside County, but I would gladly relocate if I get this job."

Belknap stood up, extended his hand, and told Nikolai, "Best of luck with the rest of the process, son," and escorted him to the door.

He walked out, and Glass, who was standing by the door the whole time walked past him and told him to wait down the hall. Glass stayed back a moment and asked, "Well, Chief, that didn't take long, what did you think?"

Belknap patted Glass on the back and told him to fast-track Drew as fast as possible. "We don't want to miss out on that kid."

Glass nearly jogged to get to Nikolai. "Follow me to my office, kid, let's go over a few things."

They walked into the bullpen and sat at Glass's desk. "Well, how did you feel it went?" Glass asked.

Nikolai thought for a moment then responded, "Not sure. The Chief asked me two questions, got up, shook my hand, and told me good luck with the rest of the process."

Glass laughed and said, "Well, he loves ya, kid. He just told me to fast-track you and snag you before anyone else does. He must have been impressed!"

CHAPTER
SIX

Back in today's world, the next morning at 0700 hours, Corporal Picarone entered Nikolai's hospital room with a shit-eating grin on his face. He shut the door, pulled up a chair, and poured himself a cup of coffee. "Kid, you are not gonna believe what has developed since we talked yesterday."

Nikolai had a worried look on his face and joked, "Well, are you gonna spill or do I have to beat it out of you?"

Sitting back in his chair, Picarone relayed the story. "Yesterday afternoon, a call came in that someone found three dead gangbangers in an apartment in Pacoima. Officers responded and found the door ajar, three men sitting on a couch and chair all shot in the head. There was a message spray painted in Spanish on the wall: *esto es lo que les pasa a las traidoras* meaning 'this is what happens to traitors.'"

Nikolai shrugged. "What does this have to do with me, ace?"

Picarone continued. "Well, detectives rolled in, and it seems that a witness saw a '65 Impala lowrider with five occupants was seen leaving the scene about twenty minutes before your shooting. After doing a little digging, an informant said that there was a hit on these three douchebags for skimming dope and drugs from Pacoima Trece. They interviewed the four remaining occupants of the car you pulled over, and one of the knuckleheads confessed to executing the contract on the three that were found. You, my friend, are lucky to be alive. Now, if you're ready to get out of this place, I am here to give you a ride to the station."

Nikolai put on his uniform pants, t-shirt and boots. Just then, Doctor Nelson came in and lectured him on taking it easy for a few days. Nikolai said he didn't feel that would be an issue as he could barely move and had had a tremendously challenging time getting his boots on and an even worse time lacing up his boots. As Picarone drove them to the station, he told Nikolai that he would just pull around back so he could slip into the locker room, change, and then head home. He reminded Nikolai not to say anything about the shooting to anyone and to try to slip in and out without anyone seeing him. Nikolai agreed.

Nikolai moved slowly as he approached the back door. He unlocked the door and walked in, speeding up his pace and slipping into the men's locker room, which happened to be close to the back door of the facility. He unlocked the locker, undressed, and put on his workout gear, slipped on his tennis shoes, and removed his badge, name tag, and other miscellaneous items from his uniform. He grabbed his war bag with one hand, dirty uniform with the other, and headed to the back door. As he walked out, the day shift Sergeant called out to him. Nikolai stopped and thought, *Damn it.*

Sergeant Brodie (nicknamed Sergeant Nutty) jogged up, patted Nikolai on the back, and said, "I just wanted to tell you what a great job you did. Everyone's talking about how you handled that shooting, kid. Anyway, enjoy the days off and feel better, eh!"

———

He walked out back and unlocked the '69 El Camino. Poor old thing needed paint and some rally wheels. She looked mean with the center lines off Nikolai's Chevelle, but once she was finished being restored, those wheels would need to be returned to their rightful owner. He got in, fired up engine, and thundered away. *She may not look sexy, but she is a great car,* he thought to himself. All the way home

Nikolai's head filled with thoughts of the last two days, and he pondered what could have been and how through training, instinct, or just pure survival skill he managed to survive an incident that could have very well taken his life. He thanked God for his weapons training, thanked God for all the years of being around his law enforcement family and hearing their stories of tragic situations, thanked God for his bulletproof vest, but mostly, he just thanked God!

He pulled up in the driveway, put the El Camino in Park, and walked inside. He slid open the patio door to let the breeze in. He turned on the radio, removed the bottle of Johnnie Walker Black the LA Sheriff Detective gave him, and poured two shots neat.

Sitting on the patio, he pondered the difference of using ice on a good scotch and how it was a cardinal sin as he took a sip, neat versus on the rocks and chuckled. "Pretty damn good," he whispered. Neither Jake or his sister Sheri were home, which was probably a good thing, he didn't want to end up sharing the events of the last few days with anyone.

He pondered calling someone but knew if he called his mother, she would lose her mind and demand he quit, and if he called his father, he would never hear the end of the stories of his years on the job. Nope, he was gonna have to keep this one to himself, realizing that no matter what he said, who he told, it would just cause more damage than good.

What good would it do to share this anyway? Just then the song by Neil Diamond, "Solitary Man" came on the radio, and Nikolai laughed again. *Cheers, God, messages come in strange ways!*

The phone rang. Nikolai picked it up after the second ring.

"Nikolai," the voice on the other end said sternly, "it's Chief Belknap."

"Hey Chief, what can I do for you."

"Well, you can get a paper and pen and write down this name and number."

Nikolai went to the kitchen counter and picked up his pen by his notepad that was usually full of items needed from the grocery store. "Go ahead, Chief," he said.

"Give Linda Wallmaker a call. She's a psychiatrist for the department. She has you penciled in for an interview tomorrow morning at ten. Call her and confirm the appointment. It's important, kid. When you're done, come by the station and see me."

"You got it, Chief, thanks."

Nikolai hung up then quickly called the number given for the psychologist and confirmed the appointment with the office staff. Just as he was about to hang up, the call waiting alert came over, and he clicked over to the incoming line. It was Picarone checking in on him. At the end of the conversation, he asked if Nikolai needed anything. Nikolai said, "Yes, a time machine, would like to either move forward to the end of this mess or go back in time so I can just avoid the whole damn thing altogether."

"I hear ya. It's a process," Picarone said.

Nikolai paused, feeling a bit overwhelmed. "Thanks, man. I appreciate you. See you tomorrow."

CHAPTER
SEVEN

The morning came too soon. Nikolai slept well again, no dreams reliving the shooting, no guilt, nothing. He was beginning to feel bad for not feeling bad. He did repeat to himself that the fucker did try to kill him; there is the quick and the dead. He made a protein shake and worked out in his gym/guest room listening to *4* by Foreigner, one of his favorite albums. The workout today was chest and triceps, which was interesting given the fractured sternum. He lay on the flat bench and did ten reps with the forty-five pound bar, no plates on either side. He felt the sting of the fracture and decided that was enough, figured he should probably actually listen to the doctors and take some time away from the gym.

Nikolai grabbed his war bag, which contained clean clothes, hygiene items, blow dryer, and the usual toothbrush and hygiene items he always carried and walked out to his El Camino. The drive to his psych appointment was taken up with his speed Spanish course on tape, which he had been listening to for six months. It was working, however. He was picking it up, and with the help of some of his brother officers speaking to him only in Spanish, it was coming along faster than he anticipated.

Parking was fun, thank god he got there early! Finally, a spot opened up about a block away. Nikolai jogged to the building, walked in, and checked in with the receptionist. He had only been waiting a moment when Wallmaker walked out and called his name. Nikolai stood up. "Yes ma'am."

She motioned to him, and they made their way back to her office, where he sat on a couch and she sat in a leather chair with a notepad in hand. It wasn't the leather couch he expected where he was to lie down and spill all his sins like in the movies, just a small office with a desk, a library of books, some simple plaques, and "the couch." Wallmaker asked a lot of questions, mostly about Nikolai's parents, siblings, pets, and personal life. He told her about his parents being divorced when he was twelve, his sister who was three years his junior, and of course his mother who was the rock for him and his sister when the marriage dissolved. He had no pets, no wife, an on and off again girlfriend, and a love of muscle cars and physical fitness.

Wallmaker told Nikolai, "Well, you are a balanced

young man. You have hobbies, you love family, and you love to work. You aren't a stressed-out, overthinking kind of person and seem to be handling the events of the shooting well. When you leave here today, you will need to go down the hall and take the MMPI test. Are you familiar with it?"

Nikolai smiled. "Oh, yes, ma'am. I've taken about a dozen of them when applying for the academy as well as law enforcement jobs."

Wallmaker chuckled. "They are fun, aren't they. Anyway, Nikolai, take the exam and you can head out. I will have my secretary set your next appointment as you head out. Do you have any questions for me?"

"Yes ma'am, what is the next step in the process?"

Wallmaker walked Nikolai to the door and down the hall. "It's pretty simple. Once you take the MMPI, I will evaluate you again and see where you are from there. Based on that, you will either be cleared for duty, or will be set up for more therapy. Your mindset will determine the timeline."

Nikolai sat down in the white five by five room with the door closed. He answered the repetitious questions. Apparently the test maker thought it would be cute to word a question seven different ways. After about three and a half hours, he walked out and turned the test in to the receptionist.

"Ma'am I have another meeting with Dr.

Wallmaker, and she said you would have a date set for me?"

The receptionist, a girl of about twenty with long black hair smiled at Nikolai and said, "Yes officer, you need to be here next Monday at the same time." She handed him a card with the doc's name on it with the appointment time and date.

Back at the station, Picarone found Nikolai sitting in the report room and put his arm around Nikolai's neck as if to put him in a choke hold. "How did it go, pal? Don't tell me, your elevator doesn't go all the way to the top, right?"

Nikolai laughed. "No man, I am good, I had to take that fuckin' MMPI for the billionth time, and I have another appointment next Monday at the same time. If I'm not nuts now, I may be by the time all this shit is done!"

Picarone laughed. "Yeah, that damn MMPI is a real pain in the ass. So, you are meeting the Chief today. He's gonna assign you to dispatch, so you'll be workin' and staying fresh with the 10 code and procedures. Truth is, runnin' the desk will be good experience for you. It'll probably help you become better at understanding what everyone else is seeing or hearing when you're in the field talking to them and trying to get your point across."

Nikolai laughed and responded sarcastically, "Dispatch, holy shit, that oughta be a blast! All bullshit aside, I'm just glad to still have a job."

Picarone patted him on the back, and as they walked to the Chief's office, he asked, "Have you contacted Payne to set up the meeting with Detective Schilochian yet?"

"No, I'll page him when I get out of the meeting with the Chief. I am honestly good to go anytime."

Picarone walked away as they got to the Chief's office. "I gotta split, man. Every damn time I get near admin, I feel like I am gonna spontaneously combust. Be cool."

Nikolai walked up to the Chief's secretary window. "Good afternoon, ma'am, can you let the Chief know Nikolai Drew is here for his two o'clock please."

Celeste was in her fifties, and she had worked for the department since she was twenty. She had seen it all, everything from being a dispatcher to a jailer to working as the Detective Bureau Secretary. She was selected by the Chief to be his secretary and had been doing that for ten years. She smiled at Nikolai. "Of course, let me ring him. Grab a seat, and I'll let you know when you can head in."

Nikolai sat down and read a *People* magazine, he wasn't really reading it, merely killing time. Five minutes later, Celeste slid the window open and waved Nikolai to the window. As he approached, Celeste said, "Have you ever noticed your hire date on your ID?"

Nikolai looked up and after a moment he said, "No ma'am, I can't say I have."

She laughed, well, you inherited your uncle's badge, right?"

"Yes ma'am, number 119. It's an old number seeing how the badges are in the four digits now."

She smiled. "You should have a look at your date of hire on your ID." She slid the window closed.

Nikolai went back to his seat and had started to pull out his wallet when the Chief himself walked out and told him to come in. As Nikolai approached the door, the Chief shook his hand, put the other on his shoulder, and escorted him through the door.

The Chief sat on a couch in front of his desk, not behind his desk, meant to relax the guest. If the Chief sits behind the desk, it means he's talking to you as the Chief and you may not like what's coming. He offered Nikolai a seat. They eyed one another for a moment. The Chief leaned forward, elbows resting on his thighs, clasping his hands together and said in a tone of concern, "How are you doing, son? Did your first interview with psych today go well?"

Nikolai thought for a moment and told the Chief, "I am good sir, and yes, I met with her. We had our first appointment today. We talked about a lot of things, and I took that godforsaken MMPI test again."

The Chief laughed. "Yeah, that thing is a killer. You look good, and the report I received from Wallmaker this morning was positive. Do you want to come back to work, or do you need a few more days to yourself?"

Nikolai responded immediately, "Put me to work as soon as you can, Chief, I'm not good sitting on my hands."

The Chief laughed again. "I like your attitude, son, just like your uncle Jim."

Nikolai huffed. "Yes sir, the man was more like a father to me than an uncle. I am certain a lot of him rubbed off on me."

The Chief told him, "So, starting tomorrow at three, I want you to suit up and work as a backup dispatcher. Will be good for you. I will put the memo forward to the PM Watch Commander. I am sure you will get through the psych thing, and we can get you back on the streets soon, if that's what you want?"

Nikolai looked at Belknap with determination and said, "Chief, there is nothing I want more, I was born for this. I didn't go through hell to get here just to lie down after the first bump in the road."

Chief Belknap smiled, stood up, and pointed at the door as he walked behind his desk and said, "Alright, get the fuck out of my office, I have important Chief shit to do." The Chief ushered him out the door, laughing.

Nikolai was smiling as he made his way down the hall to Internal Affairs and found Picarone meandering around the halls. Lou put his arm around Nikolai's shoulder and walked him down the hall away from Internal Affairs and asked, "Well, how did it go with El Jefe?"

Nikolai shrugged and said, "Good. It's like you said, I am piloting the desk till IA and Psych are done with me."

Picarone elbowed him in the ribs and said, "Well, I have some good news for ya, brother. I just left IA, and the word is, they are clearing you of any wrongdoing on the shooting, not that we thought it would go any other way. Once you are wrapped up with Psych and your sternum is good to go, you will be ready to continue training. Now, you can't be sayin' a word about any of this, okay? Just be cool and mellow and humble until we get you back to work. We gotta get you through training and probation."

Nikolai breathed a little easier. "Well damn, man. Thanks for letting me know, I was afraid they would find a way to use it to get rid of me."

Picarone laughed. "Brother, you couldn't be further from the truth. Everyone has your back on this one because it's clean, and so are you. You're the poster boy for the department at the moment. Don't fuck it up."

Nikolai smiled and paused for a moment then looked back at Picarone. "I need to have a talk with McNamara. I haven't seen him or spoken with him since the shit show. How do I reach him?"

Picarone looked at him pensively. "You need to

keep to yourself during the hearing session. McNamara has pulled his pin and retiring over this. The reality is, you need to steer clear from one another until the dust has settled and you are cleared of wrongdoing. Once that is done, I'll give you his phone number myself, and we can all get a drink and sort this shit out."

Nikolai frowned and nodded in agreement. As they walked out the back door to the parking area, Picarone patted him on the back. "I'll see you at 1500 tomorrow, kid."

CHAPTER
EIGHT

Nikolai arrived at the station at 1300 hours, walked into the gym, turned on the lights and the music, and did a light workout. Every move felt painful, but he could feel himself getting better every day. After a decent back and chest routine, he got in two miles on the treadmill then got into the shower. He got his shave done, trimmed his mustache, and took a blow dryer to what little hair he had. As he put on his uniform pants, socks, and polished Danner boots, he breathed deeply and felt thankful to be alive. He stood, put on a white t-shirt and tucked it in.

He took out the uniform shirt from the day of shooting and poked his fingers through the holes left in it. He removed his badge from the shirt, as well as his name plate, notepad, and pens from the shirt pocket, and carefully arranged them on the clean shirt. He pulled the shirt on and zipped it up. The zipper was installed for ease and to keep the shirt looking tight and professional. Nikolai had also had the shirts tailored to sew in the military creases. He tucked the shirt in, zipped up and buttoned his slacks, and cinched up his belt. He then went about cleaning and polishing his Sam Browne and all the gear. He placed his keepers in place, two in the rear between his cuff cases, two on each side in the front, and one more behind where his holster rests. He realized he had not received his weapon back from evidence, so he went to roll call without it.

Nikolai was striking in uniform: small waist, huge shoulders and chest, and arms that were well over nineteen inches around. Grabbing the shift log, he sat in the front of the room and got caught up on the events of the last seventy-two hours in the city. Typical goings on, four drive-by shootings, one street robbery, four grand theft autos, and a couple domestic violence calls. One thing did catch his eye: a bank robbery, 5' 11" male, all dark clothing wearing a white fedora, and a black sport coat with a silver tie. According to the notes, the man was slender in build, polite, and held his right hand at his waist exhibiting a handgun. He had told the teller softly to get all the money she could, no dye packs, and hand it over or he was going to execute her and anyone who got in his way. The clerk hit the panic button, units were on scene within three minutes, and poof, no car, no suspect, nothing! The guy may as well have been a ghost.

The watch commander walked in, Sergeant Brown. He patted Nikolai on the shoulder. "How ya holdin' up, kid?"

Nikolai smiled. "As good as can be expected, Sarge! Just getting everything done that needs to get done so I can get back to work, ya know?"

Sergeant Brown sighed. "I hear ya. Anything worth talking about on the log? I've been off for a few days."

Nikolai stood up and pointed at the log entry. "Just this bank robbery deal. Guy is in, he's out, gets like 20k, and vanishes."

Sergeant Brown chuckled. "Yeah, the Gentleman Bank Robber! Fuckin' guy whispers and according to like three tellers, looks like he is wearing makeup or a mask or something, always wears gloves, never leaves prints, and never draws attention. He's hit four banks in the last couple of months. He will fuck up eventually. Let's just hope he doesn't get anyone killed. Anything else?"

"Nah, Sarge, just the usual stuff," Nikolai said.

Everyone sat down for roll call, and Sergeant Brown asked for unit choices. The senior officer got to pick first. Goldy took Unit 25, typically regarded as one of the newer units in the fleet, but mostly the fastest. There were four single-man units, three two-man units total, and the Sergeant barked out the unit designations:

"L-22 Forster (Pacoima)
A-23 Sorelson and Vasquez (Sylmar)
A-24 Hunter and Villanueva, you got the Rock tonight
L-25 Goldy, you get Arleta
A-26 Big George and Hooper, you two get Pacoima
L-27 Rawlins, you a Rover tonight
L-28 is Synirine, you are our second Rover for the evening
L-20 our K-9 is out and about already and is working till 0400 hours."

Let's hit it, folks, two tickets a piece, and let's not do anything too exciting tonight. I have a headache.

After roll call, there were a few calls backed up. Nikolai had never worked dispatch before, so he just watched in the beginning. Gonzalez put out the first couple of calls. "L-22, see the woman, 415 man trying to get in the front door of her apartment, 3231 Dronfield St., Unknown description male appears to be 647 F (drunk in public), A-23 respond to back."

"L-22 control, 2 minutes out, is the suspect still in front? L-22, confirmed, I am still on the phone with the RP (reporting party). Suspect is still at the front door."

Moments later, 22 arrived on scene, parking two houses away, blacked out and approaching quietly. A-23 is 97 (10 code abbreviation for 10-97, arrived at scene).

All three officers approached quietly viewing the Hispanic male pounding on the front door of the residence. "Lucia, come on baby, let me in, I forgot my key baby!"

Forster calmly walks up, has the suspect put his hands on his head, and pats him down.

"Do you have any weapons friend, no guns, knives, small nuclear weapons?"

Suspect laughs and is clearly intoxicated. "No, man, I'm just tryin' to get inside and go to bed. The bitch won't let me in!" A-23, units are Code 4 at this time (meaning all is under control). Forster retrieved the man's identification, and they sat him on the curb at the street.

Looking at the driver's license, the man is at the right address, wrong street—he's two blocks away. Forster runs the man for warrants which come back clean. They opt to take the man home and drop him with his wife rather than arrest him for being drunk in public. A-23 offers to transport so Forster can share the story of what they discovered with the homeowner who made the call. She was quite relieved.

"L-22 control, all units are 10-8, one HBD (has been drinking), returned to his correct address two blocks away, and the RP on this call was advised and is grateful to our quick response, ma'am."

Dispatch responded, parroting the unit's response. "Roger, L-22 and A-23 are 10-8."

Around 5:30, a couple reserve police officers came in to suit up and stop by the Sergeant's office to check in. Both were old guards and had been around for twenty plus years. Cafaro is a chiropractor, and Garcia is a well-known sound man for the movie industry going back as far as Barnaby Jones, Cannon, and Vegas in the 70s. They are laughing as the Sergeant is harassing them. They all walk up to dispatch laughing, and Sergeant Brown says, "Nikolai, give me the lineup please. Okay, looks like we have your pick of Synirine or Rawlins tonight, who wants who?"

Cafaro mouths off first. "Well, I guess since Nikolai isn't free, I'll ride with that queer Big George." He laughs to himself, and Garcia slaps him.

"Don't be such an asshat, ya Wop."

Cafaro says, "I'll ride with Rawlins, Sarge. Garcia can ride with that panty waste Synirine. Ha, the only observation you're gonna get tonight Garcia is Synirine's nose hairs while he's snoring!"

The entire time, Sergeant Brown is rolling his eyes and shaking his head. "Nikolai, call the units in for their partners, would ya please? And you two numbnuts, try not to be your usual selves tonight, will ya please?"

Nikolai put it out over the air. "Unit 27, Unit 28, 10-19 partners at your convenience per L-30." Units acknowledged immediately.

———

Garcia and Cafaro suited up, and before going out, Garcia walked back up to dispatch and pulled Nikolai aside. "How ya doin', kid, you okay after all this shit?"

Nikolai stood up from behind the desk. "I am doin' better than I deserve, Vince, thank you!"

Garcia smiled, "Well, I want to extend you an offer. Please don't share this with anyone, okay? Warner Brothers studio is looking for some extras on *Hunter* and *Baywatch*, nothing special, just consistent walk-on, fill in parts. You interested? It pays well."

Nikolai almost jumped out of his boots. "Hell yes, who do I have to kill?"

Garcia wrote down a name and number. "This is Jill's direct number with the extra company, Call the Cops. Call her tomorrow afternoon, I'll let her know you will be reaching out. Say nothing to no one, kid. I really don't need anyone up my ass on this. Everyone is always asking me to make them a Hollywood star and shit. I owe your uncle a bunch, and you're a great kid, so, shhh."

Nikolai grinned again. "Thanks, Vince. With all

the shit I've been through lately, this really makes my day!"

Vince grinned. "Kid, you have some moxie. What you did out there was pretty damned amazing! I've been sharing the story with a couple of the actors and producers, and they just wanna rub elbows with a guy like you. This could be a good thing for you. You deserve something special after that, and if I can help, it's my pleasure. Now fuck off, and make sure you don't give us any shit calls tonight, okay, just good shit so the clown I am riding with doesn't fall asleep!"

Back at the desk, Nikolai noticed another reserve pull into the back gate late. Sully walked into the back, and Nikolai could see him head to the men's locker room. Nikolai walked to the watch commander's office and leaned in. "We have another late arrival, Sarge."

Sergeant Brown looked up. "Who is it?"

Nikolai said, "It's Sully, just walked in."

Sergeant Brown cheered up. "Well, that works well. He usually likes to work alone anyway. Set him up as a rover."

Nikolai walked back to the locker room and used the bathroom. While in the urinal he shouted out, "Hey Sully, how ya doin' man?"

Sully walked around the corner and used a stall across from Nikolai. "Life is good man, you recovering okay after the shooting?"

Nikolai scoffed. "Well, I am still here and going through the process. It seems to take on a life of its own. I have gone from being grateful to be alive, afraid I am going to be fired, to now just wondering what the fuck is next! Crazy, right?"

Sully was a little white in the face and seemed distracted. He was one of the few level one reserve officers, meaning he could ride alone in a patrol car just like a regular police officer and handle calls like one. He was known for being the owner of "Carpeteria" the name, the master franchise holder and all, though it had suffered over the last few years.

Nikolai asked if he was okay.

"Yeah, the wife and I had a little tiff this afternoon. You know how it is. She seems to always be pissed about somethin'. Either I am working too much, or I'm not workin' enough! I swear to god man, I think I should have never gotten married."

Nikolai laughed. "I have no clue how it is, and I hope I never do!"

The two men walked to the sink and washed their hands. Sully looked at Nikolai and smiled. "Kid, you are money to this department. You are smart, talented, and you have a good heart. You are the holy grail of what people are looking for in this line of work. You have a great career waiting for you. Ride this out, and trust me, you're gonna be fine!"

Nikolai grinned. "Thanks, man, I appreciate your insight. You are working an L-Unit as a rover tonight by the way, cool? Just get your head clear of that domestic shit before you head out. Hang out at the desk for a bit if you like."

Sully smiled. "Yes, man. Rover sounds good, see you in a bit!"

The rest of the shift was pretty quiet. Working the desk seemed right up there with watching paint dry. Nikolai bailed out early. Rather than getting cocktails with the gang, he opted to go home and get some sleep.

CHAPTER
NINE

Two weeks had gone by since Vince Garcia asked Nikolai to call Jill with Call the Cops. He wanted to get through the next Psych interview and make sure his mental health was coming along before he did like Vince asked. It was Monday morning, and Nikolai wrapped up his latest interview with his psychologist, Dr. Wallmaker. She sent him away with a clean bill of health, assuring him that she would be recommending he return to full duty.

Nikolai arrived back at the police station feeling much more confident after this morning's appointment, and he decided to give Jill a call. When she answered the phone, it caught him off guard. Jill was pleasant, sounded cute over the phone, and Nikolai found himself stuttering for a moment and couldn't manage to get his mind and mouth to work in unison. He regained his composure and was surprised that Jill made time for him to come in the same day. She asked him to show up in a uniform with no patches on it so she could get a photo of him in case the interview went well.

Nikolai arrived at the Capitol Record building on Vine in Hollywood at 11 a.m., took the elevator to the third floor, and asked for Jill. There were a few people in front of him. A female in a green uniform was sitting next to an empty seat, so he approached.

"Anyone sitting here?" he asked.

She smiled. "No, it's all yours." He opened the book he'd been reading, a book on philosophy and stoicism.

The woman asked what he was reading, and Nikolai showed it to her. "It's called *The Emperor's Handbook.* It's about stoicism and leadership, all from the interpretation and writings of Marcus Aurelius."

She introduced herself. "I'm Liz Doherty, I'm with LA Sheriff's Department by the way. So, how is the book?"

Nikolai shook her hand. "It's a little dry, but full of meaning. Lots to digest. I'm Nikolai by the way, with LAPD. You here applying for the extra gig, Liz? It sounded like fun, so I thought I would check it out."

"Yes, I am."

At that moment, the woman at the desk called Nikolai's name, and he stood. A woman walked out of one of the offices and escorted him down the hall to her office. She offered Nikolai a seat and introduced herself as Jill. She was 5'10", slender, in her mid to late 40s, and breathtakingly attractive.

"Have a seat, Nikolai. Do you have your resume with you?" He handed it to her as he sat down. As she read his bio, Jill asked Nikolai to tell her his story.

"Well, I'm a sixth-generation law man and have been in this trade for about a year, including my time spent in the academy. I have a history of acting in Junior High and High School. I have many years of experience with martial arts of one form or another and remain very physically active."

———

Jill smiled. "I can see that here. You come highly recommended. Vince Garcia says you are one hell of a cop, and that you're funny and a good guy to be around. We are looking for people who aren't bent on ego and can just go with the flow on set. A lot of this is just walking around as a fill-in with no lines. Sometimes we call on extras for speaking parts; though not often, that usually leads to a SAG card. Do you know what that is?"

Nikolai responded, "Yes ma'am, Screen Actors Guild card."

Jill barked, "Stand up, let me get a look at you. Hmmm, 6'2", about 220?"

Nikolai smiled. "You're good. I'm 6'2", 230, ma'am."

Jill asked if the job was something that sounded like he would be interested in, explaining that it paid $25.00 per hour, minimum four hours a day.

Nikolai responded joyfully, "Yes ma'am, sounds like it would be a fun adventure, and the money is just right." After all, Nikolai was making $19.00 per hour, so this was like a pay raise.

Jill stood up and walked to her office door. "Alright, Nikolai, let's go down the hall, and I'll get a couple shots of you for the book, and we will get you started. How this works is, you will get a page. When you do, call back immediately—these gigs are first come, first serve. If you don't call back and can't work this into your schedule more than three times, you will likely get to the Dropped Candidate List. If you respond quickly and fill the need, you will likely be quite busy. Does that make sense?"

She escorted him to a small room with photography equipment and introduced Nikolai to the photographer. A couple quick shots of the front and each side, and it was all over, quick and painless. Nikolai expressed his appreciation for the opportunity and let her know that he wouldn't let her down.

Nikolai left the building and headed into the station. He rushed into the locker room, got changed into his gym clothes so he could get in a workout before his shift started. He made a pre-workout drink, walked in the gym, and began the drill. It was back and triceps day with a mix of cardio and abs. Three hundred reps on each body part as well as three intervals of one and a half miles running before, in the middle, and after the workout. This would take about two hours and give Nikolai time to go out, grab a quick lunch, then head back in to shower before work. The music was loud and usually contained some Sammy Hagar, Van Halen, AC/DC, and Black Sabbath. Nothing pumps the heart rate up like a little "Dirty Deeds" by AC/DC!

As the workout wound down, Nikolai opted for some non-salted cashews for lunch. While eating, a page came over the intercom: "Drew to L-50's Office, Drew to L-50's Office." Nikolai secured his gear and locker and jogged to the office, where the secretary escorts him in.

The Chief came around the desk and offers Nikolai a seat back in front of the desk again. Chief Belknap smiled. "How are you doin' today, son?"

Nikolai replied, "Good, Chief, sorry for the clothes. I was in the gym when the shout came over the intercom, and didn't want to make you wait."

Chief smiled. "Well, I figured you would be here early. You always are. Wanted to go over the findings of the psych eval. with you personally; it just came in."

Nikolai leaned back and must have turned sheet-white because the Chief leaned forward and smiled, slapped Nikolai's knee, and said, "Relax, son, you are cleared for duty. Clean shoot, clean written, and the psych doc found you genuine, kind, and in her opinion the perfect cop. Now, I have you with the next FTO starting tonight if you are ready."

Nikolai stood up, grinned, and said, "Hell yes, Chief. Is there anything else?"

"No, son. Glad to have you back in the field. Have a great shift and be safe."

As he walked out and down the hall, Nikolai was elated and thrilled. Nikolai stopped short of the hall leading to the locker room just in time to avoid being run over by Sully who was walking nearly at a trot. "How ya doin, mister?"

Sully was in a rush, didn't apologize. He was clearly in a hurry to get to his locker.

"Hey, brother, you okay?" Nikolai offered in a happy tone as he started to go about shaving.

No response from Sully for a few moments, then Sully shouted back at Nikolai, "I'm good man, just gotta get my shit together then call my wife before I begin shift. I swear, Nikolai, you need to avoid the whole getting married thing as long as you can. Just work, travel, and raise hell. Trust me, you will appreciate that advice later in life."

Nikolai laughed back and said, "Well, brother, trust me, my mom told me a couple simple things when I was growing up. She said, 'Before getting married know this, the woman you would have at twenty, you wouldn't have at thirty, and so on.' And, 'Before you ever decide to have children, be sure you know one thing. Children are the weapon some women will use to destroy men!'"

Sully laughed so hard and out loud it rattled the locker room. "Jesus, man, your mom is sure locked on!"

Nikolai responded, "Well she lived on both ends of it, brother. I got to see it first hand. She was a single parent making ends meet for my sister and I and watched her brother get victimized by his evil wife for decades. I think in reality, she regrets marrying my dad, and in truth, she told me as much as she loves me and my sister, she wished she had made better choices."

Nikolai looked around the corner at Sully who was fidgeting about and suddenly looked up like a squirrel who just heard a hunting animal about to attack.

"You sure you're okay, brother?" Nikolai asked.

Sully took a deep breath and calmed himself, sat, pulled his uniform pants on. After a moment, he looked up at Nikolai and smiled. "Yeah, brother, just can't wait to get in the field. This job is like a release, simply makes me feel good to be here, and all my normal life is left at the door when I walk it, ya know what I mean?"

Nikolai smiled. "Yeah, man, I get it." He got his own uniform on.

After the shooting, Nikolai decided to dump the department issued Smith and Wesson 645 and bought a Sig Sauer P-220, .45. He had shot one of the other officer's Sig and was impressed. It was lighter and felt easier to manipulate. He of course had to go through the range master to qualify with the weapon before taking it out on duty. He had plenty of time to do so during his time off. Nikolai removed the magazine, examining the seven rounds within, pulled back the slide, and ejected the hollow point round.

He slowly slid the magazine back into the weapon, felt the click securing it, pulled the slide back jacking a live round into the chamber, hit the de-cocking lever dropping the hammer safely, and slid the weapon in the holster.

He removed the magazine again, placed the ejected round back in, and slid the magazine back into the weapon. He then removed the other magazines from his belt, all three, and checked them to ensure they were all full. Grabbing his posse box, he headed to roll call.

As he walked into the squad room, he walked quietly and kept to himself. Nikolai placed his posse box on the front row table and looked at the bulletins for today, checking who was wanted, hot spots for criminal conduct, and took some notes. He sat down and waited, reflecting on everything that had brought him to this point. Sergeant Brown walked in and laid some paperwork on the podium, looked up, and acknowledged Nikolai. "Hey kid, come in my office for a moment."

He led Nikolai into his office and looked him over. "Chief says you are good to go and has me resuming your training tonight. You sure you're up to it?"

Nikolai responded quickly and enthusiastically that he was ready to go and couldn't wait to get back in the saddle. Sergeant Brown smiled. "Glad to hear it, we're moving forward with the next phase of training, I am pairing you with Shelldrake. He's tough but fair; he's gonna probably push you a little to make sure you are not just bullshitting the psych to get back to work. If you need anything, let me know alright?" Nikolai nodded and acknowledged him and walked back into the squad room.

They walked into roll call and took their positions as the crew made their way into the room. Shelldrake called out to Nikolai, "Come back here, kid. I don't sit in the front, that's for rookies."

As he sat next to Shelldrake, Sergeant Brown barked, "Before we get started, let's all welcome Officer Drew back to patrol. He passed his shooting review and psych evaluation. Sadly, he's stuck with Shelldrake, but I have a feeling if he can dodge a bullet, this won't be that big a challenge!" He dished out unit assignments, and Drew and Shelldrake walked their gear to their unit. Drew got their assigned shotgun, confirmed the weapon was clear of any ammunition, then got the unit loaded up. He then did a review of the unit's condition and made the appropriate notes and reported what he found to Shelldrake.

Shelldrake nodded. He placed his foot on the rear bumper of the unit and said, "Let's chat for a moment, shall we?"

Nikolai nodded. Shelldrake said quietly, "I have read your file and reviews so far. You seem to have a solid grasp on everything but report writing and memorizing the city streets, sound about right?"

Nikolai responded quickly, "Yes sir."

The training officer smiled. "Alright, son, let's get to work and see what the real deal is. The best way for me to work out your kinks is to take you for a test run. For the record, I respect what you went through. Hell, most would have choked, shit themselves, and quit the job—if they survived it. My job is to push you and make sure you are still cut out for this shit, understood?"

Nikolai looked the man in the eye, though he was slightly shorter than Shelldrake, and said, "Sir, I wouldn't have it any other way!"

Shelldrake smiled and pointed at the driver door. "Alright kid, you're drivin', let's roll, first up, get me to 146. I need some coffee!" This was a test, Nikolai knew. The training officer would give the trainee merely the number portion of the address of one of three 7-11's where officers regularly went to get free coffee. The boot, or trainee, best get that right and best get the training officer his coffee—and best know the fastest way to get there before anything else! Drew fired up the unit, pulled out, and got them to 146 in just a matter of moments. So far the radio had been quiet, meaning no calls for service, so the two got coffee and stood at the back of the unit, which Nikolai strategically backed into the parking spot.

Shelldrake sipped his coffee and breathed out happily, "Okay, probie, let's talk about the difference between proactive and reactive police work. What is the difference? Keep the answer simple for me so I don't have to slap the shit outta you, okay?" Shelldrake grinned over his hot cup of coffee.

Nikolai responded as quickly as possible, "Proactive is self-initiated work based on observations and knowledge of the beat area, whereas reactive police work is merely responding to calls for service?"

Shelldrake just about dropped his coffee and smiled. "Is that it?"

Nikolai looked at him, pondered for a moment and said, "Yup, that's all I got."

Shelldrake set his coffee on the trunk lid of the unit. "Well holy shit, probie, that may very well be the best god damn answer I have ever gotten from a boot since I have been doin' this damn job! Well done!"

The first night back on patrol came and went with

several radio calls and Nikolai managing to handle everything that came at him without hesitation or appearing to be lost in the moment. The post shift discussion had Shelldrake give Nikolai a homework assignment: to look up the department's off-duty shooting policy and write an officer's report for an imaginary scenario detailing how he would handle the following:

While standing in line at a grocery store, he sees a suspect holding a weapon demanding the cash from the register. The suspect takes the cash and walks calmly out of the store. "Nikolai, you are armed, what do you do?"

"That's it," Nikolai replied.

"Have it ready when we get to roll call tomorrow, see you then," Shelldrake said.

On his way home Nikolai was contemplating several different scenarios in his head:

Put a bullet in the idiot's head and call it a day, but what if there was another suspect lurking? He could end up getting himself or others killed for just a few bucks.

Let the guy get what he came for, remember what he looks like, marks, scars, tats, height, weight etc. then calmly walk out and see which direction he went and if he got in a car, get the plate. This would work as long as the guy didn't kill or hurt anyone.

He decided to pick up the phone and call the one person he knew he could count on to shoot him straight on the matter, his uncle Bob. He hated to use the damn cell phone. It was so costly, but it was late at night and the calls were supposed to be much less expensive. He dialed the number, hit send, and after about twenty rings, finally the other end picks up. The gruff voice of his uncle Bob Smith answered the phone. "The fuck is this, it better be a god damn emergency, cause if it ain't, you may end up needin' to call 911." He coughed a little.

Nikolai spoke up. "Hey, Unc. It's me."

Uncle Bob continues, "Well, damn it kid, you better not be in jail or some shit, what the hell time is it anyway?"

He apologized and said, "It's about ten after midnight, means it's about ten after one there in El Paso; shit, I'm sorry if I woke you up, Unc."

Laughing and coughing at the same time, the retired Sheriff of Hudspeth responded, "Now kid, you know I'm always up late. What's on your mind, son?"

Nikolai told him about how training was going, never mentioning the shooting he was in, just brought up the homework assignment. Uncle Bob responded thoughtfully, "I see, well, I can see why the training officer is having you put your thoughts to paper, and both of your thoughts are solid. Frankly, I'd shoot the son of a bitch, but you're right, there are a lot of what ifs there. Out here in Texas, we'd get away with shootin' that SOB, out there in Sunny Southern California; you're liable to get sued, arrested, or both.

I would go with option two." Uncle Bob continued "You sound like you're drivin', son, on your way home from work?"

Nikolai confirmed that he was in fact on his way home.

"Well, get the hell off that damn cell phone, thing's gonna cause you to go bankrupt, develop brain cancer, or grow a third eye or maybe all of the above. I love ya, kid, let's catch up when you can call on a landline!"

Nikolai acknowledged Uncle Bob's desire to get off the phone. "Chat soon, Unc. love you too!"

He got home late, and was a Friday. He backed the El Camino into the driveway and went inside quietly so as to not wake up either of the roommates, especially his sister—family being what it is acts out a little worse than buddies. The thundering sound of the V8 starting probably managed to do that! *This hour and a half drive crap has gotta end*, he thought to himself as he turned on the TV. Still restless from the day, he turned on *The Terminator*, volume low, and began writing out his report. Two beers later, the movie was about over, and the report was completed. Thank God his printing was clean; otherwise he'd be typing this up on the IBM Correcting Selectric tomorrow before work. Although, he typed a hell of a lot faster than he wrote by hand. Three a.m., and he hit the sack—turned off the television, lay down, and was out within minutes.

At 0800 hours the next day, Nikolai woke up on his own, no alarm. Five hours of sleep apparently did the trick. Coffee was still in the pot, along with a note from his roommate Jake: *"We're goin out to meet Dan at Palomino Station tonight, see you then!"*

As he was sipping coffee and watching the news, the phone rang. "Hey, big brother, whatcha doin'?"

Nikolai replied, "Havin some coffee, you?"

His sister Sheri cheerfully responded, "Well, it's Saturday, and I'm with Mom. We're goin' over to Kountry Folks Kitchen, wanna meet up?" He agreed but made it clear it would need to be quick as he had to get in to work early.

Nikolai got in the shower and within fifteen minutes, got to Kountry Folks just in time to get his favorite seat and say hello to his favorite waitress, Janette. They had a thing, on again, off again. She was young and didn't want children and was a huge flirt. Janette smiled when she saw him. "So, Nikolai, what have you been up to these days?"

He told her that he had been consumed with work and went on about how the commute back and forth to LA was nearly killing him. She asked what he was doing when he got off work that evening. He laughed and said, "Well, I get off about midnight then headed to the Palomino Station with my roommate Jake. It's gonna be late, but fun, wanna meet us over there?"

Janette grinned. "Well, yeah, maybe I'll just be

waiting when you get there; who's meeting you for breakfast?"

Nikolai grinned thinking to himself, *Way to hand grenade a perfectly good guys night out. Sometimes I just talk too damned much.* "My mom and sister are swinging by so we can catch up."

The slender blonde waitress flipped her hair casually and said, "I'll get them over to you as soon as they get here, hun."

Moments later, they arrived. Nikolai got out of the booth and hugged his mother and sister, Mom was just a smidge shorter, and so was Sis, Mom being 6'1" and Sis at 6' even. Nikolai's 6'2" frame didn't tower over them, but his 230 pounds of muscles made him look monstrous next to the two ladies.

Sheri burst out first, "Hey, are you still thinking of moving to LA?" He'd brought up that he was tired of the drive and was seriously considering it. Sheri was so excited she could hardly stand herself.

She told him that her old boyfriend David wanted to move out there too. He had enough savings that he could spend a few months finding work. She thought the two of them would make great roommates.

Janette returned. "Do you guys know what you want?" She was grinning eagerly at Nikolai.

Mom ordered egg whites, cottage cheese, and an English muffin and coffee, Sheri ordered a veggie omelet with rye toast and coffee, and Nikolai pondered for a moment then said, "I have been craving chicken fried steak and eggs over easy, please. Hash browns, and I'll have an English muffin as well, burnt please, with a cup of coffee." Janette gallivanted off with a spring in her step.

Sheri laughed. "She still has the hots for you, ya know."

Nikolai smiled. "Well, I don't have the hots for anyone these days, just tryin' to learn the ins and outs of this damned job without getting killed or fired, or both."

Nikolai continued, "Anyway, as for Diamond Dave, that sounds like a good possibility, I have to do something, this commute is killin' me. Jake is talking about moving in with his girlfriend—that is not going to end well! Bad for him, but this is the perfect opportunity to make a change. I'll reach out to David and chat with him about it, thanks, Sis!"

Sheri smiled. "You're welcome! Now, what is going on with you and Shelly?"

Nikolai looked at his mother and sister as he took the first sip of his coffee. "Well, nothing has changed. She still comes sniffing around and has suddenly moved to Pasadena with Falcon Cable doing accounting there under Ward." Nikolai laughed and said, "She is full of drama, Sis. Honestly, I am just focusing on the job. Besides, neither one of us is serious about any form of relationship, and frankly, as Mom always puts it, I think she's in love with the idea of love, and now that I'm a cop, it's just become one hundred times worse."

His Mom chimed in, "Well, have fun and be smart honey. Best to be the chasee than the chaser, I always say. She cheated on you once and was fooling around with you while she was married. She's a drama-ridden soul and is damaged goods if you ask me."

————

Janette delivered their breakfast, and once done eating, Nikolai walked his sister and mother to their car. He gave them each a bear hug, nearly dying in pain from the fractured sternum injury. He groaned out loud. His mother pulled back and looks suspiciously at him. "You okay, hun?" she asked.

He paused for a moment. "Oh, yeah, I pulled a chest muscle while doing a heavy lift on the bench press the other day." As he walked to the El Camino, he called out to them, "Love you both, see you soon."

He unlocked the door of the El Camino, slid the key in the ignition, turned it over, and smiled when the 350 roared to life. "God damn, I love this car." He turned on the radio, and the song "Sultans of Swing" had just started! He turned the radio up, slid the column shifter into Drive, and cruised out of the parking lot feeling like a boss.

CHAPTER
TEN

Nikolai looked at his watch and realized he had time to make a stop at Bondo Bob's (Bob Brown's Auto Body) to check on his street rod that Bob Brown had been working on for the last two and a half years. The '67 Chevelle that Nikolai owned since he was fifteen and in high school that gained him tons of popularity and frankly, turned him into someone of notoriety. It would be a crapshoot, 50/50 shot if Bob was working on a Saturday. As Nikolai turned into the parking lot, he thought to himself, *Saints preserve us, he is here!*

Funny, the three shops in a row next to Bondo Bob's had parts from the damn car. Cook's Top Shop had the seats and door panels in the attic, and Paul's Cylinder Head and Machine, next door to Cook's had the stroker motor; in pieces, but it was there! Paul and John even had a damn Muncie M-22 Rock Crusher in the crate they often teased Nikolai with, offering to sell it to him from time to time!

Parking at the end, he walked down to Paul's first. They had a great conversation, talking about the heads and looking over the valve job that Paul was massaging. The heads ports were shiny and opened "Port Matched" not only to the big tube Hooker headers, but also to the Edelbrock Victor Junior intake that would sit atop the 388 stroker motor.

Old Man Cook walked out, and they talked about how magnificent the wonder sled was going to look when it was all done. Hell, they even talked about how magnificent it was going to run with the legendary 388 cubic inch stroker motor it was going to have! If, that is, Bondo Bob ever finished the damn paint! Nikolai walks down to the end, and lo and behold, found Bondo Bob actually working on the Chevelle.

"Hey, Brown, how the hell are you sir?" Nikolai asked.

Bondo Bob's hair was all messed up. He was dressed in a filthy powder blue shirt and dark blue slacks with a patch on one side that said BOB BROWN'S AUTO BODY. On the other side was a patch that said BOB. Bondo Bob smiled. "Well, kid, I am doin great, ya know. I know a fella who does this for a livin and actually makes money at it! Give me a hand pushing this piece of shit out, will ya?"

Nikolai helped him roll his own Chevelle out of

the warehouse. Bondo Bob asked him to help him take off the driver's door, and about then, Bob told Nikolai in a low voice, "Hey, some of your pals are walking up kinda sneaky, kid. May wanna be careful —that peashooter is hangin' out of your pants."

Nikolai thought to himself, *Well, fuck, I just became what I was told to never become, a rookie with a gun in his waistband!*

Nikolai turned toward the officers who were walking between cars with guns drawn, showed his badge, and apologized. The officers from Riverside PD approached slowly, took the badge, folded it back in the wallet. One officer reached for his radio, keyed the mic. "A-33 Code 4, off-duty officer, we are clear, party advised."

Nikolai apologized again, and the officer looked at him. "You must be new, kid, yes?"

Ashamed, Nikolai responded, "Yes sir, well almost a year."

The officer handed Nikolai his wallet. "Leave the gat under the seat or in your locker, Dirty Harry. Trust me, you don't wanna get blown up over being stupid." And with that he walked away with his partner. Nikolai walked over to his '69 El Camino and put the .45 under the seat, then walked back over to Bondo Bob.

Brown laughed. "Well, that's somethin' you don't experience every day!"

Nikolai made a stupid face. "Yeah, funny! So tell

me BB, how long are we lookin' before you finish up my sled! Cecil and Paul are getting tired of storing my shit."

Bondo Bob laughed. "Yeah, they let me know about every other day. Probably two or so months. We have a lot done already. Body work is done, primer is setting. I have some bushings I need to pick up for the body and so forth, but we're almost ready to lay some color, kid."

It had been over a year since Nikolai parked the car at Bondo Bob's shop, but he was legendary and worth the wait. Considered one of the best and most reasonably priced painters in the Inland Empire, or further.

"Well, that's good news, sir. I miss this old sled; it's been way too long."

Bondo Bob smiled. "I am on it like shit on a shingle, kid. Just have the money when she is done, okay?"

Nikolai smiled. "I have the money, brother, I will never leave you hangin'."

They walked over to Nikolai's '69 El Camino, and as Bob shook his hand he said, "When are you gonna let me paint this poor sled for ya?"

Nikolai looked up at him as he sat in the part primer, part blue El Camino and said, "Just as soon as you help me get that wreck back on the road! I can't leave this one with you for three years until I have another fuckin' car to drive! But I promise, you will get his one when I get that one runnin', Bob."

Nikolai started the 350, slid it into Drive, and pulled away. As he hit Jurupa from the driveway, Nikolai stuck his foot on the accelerator and lit the tires up! Both of the 275/60 15's broke loose as the posi-traction rear end did its thing.

He turned up the radio to listen to "Dirty White Boy" by Foreigner, tapping his hands on the steering wheel and thinking, *Well, if I had a theme song, guess this would be it!*

Nikolai got home just in time to take an hour or so nap before heading in to the station.

CHAPTER
ELEVEN

At 1330 hours Nikolai rolled in to the secure parking lot for the station. He walked in the back door with his war bag, which was just a gym bag full of personal hygiene gear shower shoes "because one never knows how clean that floor is" and of course, clean underwear and socks; and don't forget the loaded .45 and a couple clips full of ammo, cause ya just never know. He secured the bag in his locker and went for a run. He finished the first mile in about eight minutes. With his sternum not fully healed, every time he tried to kick the jog into a run, he felt like his chest was on fire. He got in the gym and knocked out three hundred reps of chest, incline bench superset with dumbbell flys, flat bench with the same, then decline cables super set with intervals of fifty push-ups.

He hit the street again for another mile, and this

time he's done in seven minutes, twenty seconds. The pain was a little more tolerable. He went through triceps and abdominals reps. At twenty-two, Nikolai was chiseled, not huge, but way above average. He hit the street one more time and poured on the run. This time he completed the mile in under seven minutes. Nikolai cooled down, hit the locker room, showers, shaves, fixes what little hair he has, and gets dressed.

One of the other patrolmen walked in as he was washing his shower shoes, Lense Seaman, who everyone considered an ass kissing college boy with the cop skills of Dobey Gillis, earning him the nickname Fancy Pants Lense. He walked up to the sink, looked down at the shoes, and in an attempt at a manly drill sergeant voice said, "What the fuck are you doin' washing your shoes in the sink, mister?"

Nikolai looked down at him, smiled, and said politely but with a voice that would honestly scare small children and most men, "Cleaning my shower shoes off, because one never knows what assclown pissed or worse in the shower. Before I put them back in my bag, they are being disinfected. Alright with you"—pause—"sir?"

Lense adjusted himself, walked away, and responded, "Whatever, rookie."

Nikolai got his uniform squared away, locked up his personal effects, and hung his semi-wet towel in the shower so it would be dry by the end of shift. He grabbed his posse box and headed to roll call, twenty minutes before the Sergeant ise due to arrive. He checked the previous patrol logs then went up to chat with the on duty dispatcher to see what was pressing or where the hot spots have been.

"Officer Saenz, would you care for a break, or can I bring you a cup of coffee?" Nikolai asked.

She smiled graciously. "Thank you, Nikolai. Coffee, black, would be perfect."

He returned with a cup, and she filled him in on all the juicy goings on from the last two shifts. "HTF, or High Times Familia, has some new art/graffiti in the business district; Shakin Cats have been crossing out names in San Fer Territory, and there are random sightings of drunks on the Mall; other than that, it's been pretty quiet!"

Armed with the latest intel, Nikolai knew where to look for trouble. All that was left was to see who was gonna get the smackdown laid on them tonight. Roll call began, and Sergeant Brown barked out the unit assignments. As Shelldrake and Nikolai walked out, Nikolai told Shelldrake what he had learned from dispatch and the daily log. Shelldrake grinned. "Okay, rookie, first things first. Where's my report writing assignment you owe me? After that, what do you want to tackle today? I mean, it gets dark around five, and there's supposed to be a full moon tonight. There are no radio calls backed up?"

Nikolai reached into his posse box and handed the training officer the report he requested. While Nikolai prepped the car and inspected it, Shelldrake read the report.

Shelldrake smiled. "Well done, probie, you earn the honor of driving again this evening and you can even lay on me what kind of proactive shit you would like to stir up. By the way, don't forget, we have a couple greenies to write as well." Nikolai got behind the wheel, and Shelldrake put out, "3-A-22 is 10-8!" He hung up the mic and said loudly, "Damn, I love this job!"

Dispatch responded "Roger 22, unit is 10-8."

Nikolai rolled the unit to 146, his training officer's favorite spot for coffee. They walked in, and Nikolai smiled at the clerk. "Hey, Davinder!" He hit him with a high five.

Davinder smiled and with his thick Indian accent said, "Hellooooo, buddy!" They each got a cup of coffee. Shelldrake held the cup of coffee up at the clerk, and the clerk nodded at the two men giving them the notion that the coffee is on him. As Shelldrake walked out the door, Nikolai slid a dollar bill over to Davinder, who smiled. Nikolai just couldn't take stuff for free.

He walked out to the patrol car, put his foot up on the bumper as he sipped his coffee, looked at the training officer, and said, "So, here's my idea, after the sun goes down, I was thinkin' since there are a ton of complaints about drug activity around the 500 block of Kalisher, we could hide the unit and work some stealthy foot patrol? We could wear earphones, let dispatch know what we're up to on frequency two so the dirtbags we are going to sneak up on don't know we're comin?"

Shelldrake got into the unit, sipped his coffee, and commented with a chuckle, "Foot beat, old school, I kinda dig it, kid. Let's give it a shot."

Nikolai slid in the driver's seat, smiled, and pulled out of the parking lot.

As they turned onto Hubbard Boulevard, a car ran the stop sign headed westbound on Second Street and slid to a stop, nearly hitting Shelldrake's door. The female driver had an *oh shit* look on her face and decided to turn left rather than right onto Hubbard in hopes of avoiding being contacted by the officers.

Shelldrake looked at Nikolai with a scowl on his face. "You know the rule, kid. If I nearly get killed, we gotta stop 'em, first greenie of the night!"

Nikolai turned the unit around and hit the lights just as he got up to the girl's vehicle. Nikolai reached for the radio mic and called it in.

Shelldrake was out of the unit before it even stopped, and Nikolai got out immediately thereafter and approached the vehicle. "Afternoon ma'am, my name is Officer Drew with the Los Angeles Police Department. The reason I am stopping you—"

She cut him off. "I know, officer, I ran the stop sign. I am so sorry, I wasn't paying attention and blew it. Luckily, I only nearly ran you two over."

Nikolai smiled. "Yes ma'am, luckily; may I see your license, registration, and proof of insurance please?"

She reached for the information out of her purse and her glove box. Meanwhile, Shelldrake was poised at the passenger side door of the vehicle, and Nikolai had his right hand poised on the grip of his .45, thumb on the release as he watched her fish for the documents he requested. "You don't have any guns in the car or warrants for your arrest do you, young lady?" Nikolai asked.

She handed him her documents and replied, "No sir, officer."

Nikolai retreated to the passenger side of the unit, at which time dispatch responded to the request with a report of no wants or warrants and a valid registration to an owner name Cassandra Mendoza.

Nikolai had already retrieved the citation book from the center console of the vehicle and has already begun writing a ticket as he looked over the vehicle and simultaneously responded to dispatch, "Roger control, 22 is Code 4," meaning there are no issues, no need for additional units.

Shelldrake was watching their surroundings, as Nikolai wrote the ticket. Moments later, he set the citation book on the hood of the car, approached the driver side of Cassandra's car, and asked her to please step out and join him. She did as she was requested and carefully walked back to the passenger side of the police cruiser. Nikolai tells her in the tone of a stand-up comic "Ms. Mendoza, the reason we stopped you was for failing to stop at a posted stop sign, violation of 22450 of the vehicle code. That happens to be a moving violation. I also noticed as you nearly parked your car on my partner's lap that you have no license plate on the front of your car.

"Now, I could cite you for both, but honestly ma'am, that stop sign ticket is expensive and would cause you a hike in fees for your insurance where the missing plate on the front of the car is just a fix it ticket. Because I have no desire to make the insurance industry any more money today and because beneath this badge beats a heart"—he tapped his right hand over his badge—"I am only going to write you for the fix it ticket.

"What this means, ma'am, is you merely need to get that front license plate put on, and if you can't find the one you are missing, just go to the DMV and they will issue you new plates. When you get that fixed, come by the station, and I will gladly sign this off, which will only cost about ten dollars, rather than $200.00. Just sign where the red X is. It's a promise to repair the issue in the next thirty days, ma'am."

Cassandra signed the ticket and returned the pen. Nikolai tore off her copy and escorted her back to her vehicle safely. Shelldrake put out over the radio, "3-A-22 is 10-8."

Dispatch responded, "Roger 3-A-22 is 10-8, 22,

respond to 1113 San Fernando Rd., Carter's Place regarding a 415 man who is reportedly HBD, described as a 5'9" male, black, wearing a white tank top, tan pants, and no shoes. RP reports he is in the bar and belligerent."

"A-22 Roger, 2 minute ETA."

Officer Vasquez chimed in. "3-L-24, be advised I am in the area and will be assisting the unit at 1113 San Fernando Road."

Dispatch responded, "Control copies, 24 to assist unit 22."

Vasquez got back on the radio. "24 to 22, be advised, I am standing by the rear door, when you are 97, (meaning on scene) let me know when you are walking in and I'll meet you inside."

Nikolai squeezed the call button on his handheld radio and said, "Roger 24, 3-A-22, we are walking in now."

As Nikolai and Shelldrake walked in, Shelldrake told Nikolai, "If this guy is out of control and can't be reasoned with, you go to his left. I'll take his right, and we will cuff him, got it. 24 can run interference."

"You got it, boss," Nikolai said calmly. They entered the bar. It was dimly lit, and before they walked in, they stood there a moment to let their eyes adjust.

The belligerent man was sitting against the wall on the floor at the far left side, screaming, "I swear to god, I will beat the hell outta all you mother fuckas!"

As the irate man yelled, his speech was slurred. He was dressed as described, white tank top, tan pants, no shoes, and just sitting on the floor soaked in his own piss.

Shelldrake looked at the rookie. "Well kid?"

Nikolai addressed the man. "Hey sir, you okay?" He reached down to help the man up. "Let us help you up, champ."

The man looked at the two officers. Unit 24, Vasquez, has walked in at the back and has been standing there with his hands on his hips, one of them on his hickory nightstick just in case. Vasquez walked over to the bartender, who he knew from hangin' out after work and from other radio calls. "What's this guy's deal, Casey?"

Casey laughed. "Man, I have no clue, he walked in here high as a kite and started begging for a beer. Next thing I know he's yelling, motherfuckin everyone and threatening to beat the shit out of everyone in the place if we don't give him a beer! Yeah, he's around a lot, but usually down by the wash. We will take care of it, thanks."

By now the fellas had the smelly, filthy transient handcuffed. Nikolai patted the guy down, wearing rubber gloves, since the guy's pants and lower extremities were soaked in urine. "He's clean, well, he has no weapons on him anyway," he said with a disgusted look. Nikolai removed the piss-soaked Velcro wallet from his back pocket and opened it up.

All that was in there was an expired California ID card and what appeared to be a cite release from a few days before.

Nikolai laughed. "Well, shall we get him out of this place so people can relax in peace? I have his ID." Shelldrake helped him walk the fine young man out front to the unit.

Vasquez opened the door. "Oh, your Ghetto-Limo is gonna need a serious fogging when you get this guy out, best open the window." Shelldrake rolled the back windows down and put out "22 control, unit is Code 4, 10-15 with 1 647 F enroute 10-19 with 1, thanks for the back 24!" Moments later, the two arrived at the station, pulled in the secure gate, and Nikolai backed the unit into the sally port.

Shelldrake dropped the sally port gate and handed his guns to Nikolai, who locked all of them up in the secure gun locker. The two men escorted the shoeless drunk to the holding cell, and Nikolai placed the piss-soaked wallet and ID in a plastic bag and handed it to the jailer "Sorry about this one, man!"

Mackey had been around for twenty years booking dirt bags and shrugged it off. Nikolai got Mackey's attention. "Hey, hold on for a second. Let me wash off that ID, make a copy of it, and bring it back to you so we can run him. I'll let you know in a few minutes what charges to book him for, brotha."

Nikolai walked to the restroom and washed the ID thoroughly, dried it off, and swapped out his rubber gloves. He made two copies of the ID, kept one, and gave the other to dispatch to run for warrants, then returned the clean ID to the jailer. As he walked into the report room, Shelldrake was sitting there and asked him, "So, you didn't run him in the bar, why? No right or wrong answer by the way, just curious."

Nikolai looked at him for a moment and responded, "He was abusive, drunk, and causing a scene for the business owner. I thought the first thing once we assessed him would be to get him out of there and restore peace. He had an ID and a ticket in his wallet, so I figured after patting him down, it was just as easy to get all the particulars once we got him in the station, sir."

"Good analysis, probie," Shelldrake offered. "Now the question is what do you see with this guy, under the influence?"

Nikolai looked at Shelldrake. "He's drunk, he smells of some nasty alcohol that is seeping out of his pores, but he also has some needle marks in his left arm. He's a little slow and lethargic. His pupils are constricted, and I noticed while checking his pulse standing there that it was about forty beats per minute.

"We have a choice. We can book him on the simple 647 F, drunk in public, or we can bang him for 11550 H&S and flip him into an informant so we can get to his dealer. I would prefer to get him for the H&S charge."

Shelldrake patted him on the back. "Good job, probie. Roll him up and get on the arrest report. I will get the info to the booking officer, 647 F and 11550 H&S. You may want to get the specifics you need for the report."

Nikolai walked over to booking, entered the holding cell with the prisoner, and checked his heart rate which was 38 beats per minute (normal being high 60s to 80).

Then he checked his pupil size with his certified pupil card and confirmed the suspect's pupils were approximately 1.2 mm with little to no reaction to light. He also noted the injection site and took a Polaroid of the markings on his left inner arm for evidence. During the observation work, Nikolai noticed something roll out of the pant leg of the transient. The dirtbag was still too out of it to have even noticed what was going on. Nikolai pushed the suspect's chest against the booking cell wall, reached down, and picked up a small tightly wrapped black balloon with a hard substance inside it. He had the jailer do a more thorough search on the detainee, at which time he found a syringe between the cheeks of his ass.

After writing the report, he had Shelldrake review it as well as the evidence, photo, and urine specimen he took and packaged up along with the balloon of heroin and syringe. Shelldrake patted him on the back, told him to book the evidence in, and he would turn the report into the desk.

"Nice work, probie, and fast. What do you think we should do with this guy?"

Nikolai asked, "Can we offer to throw out the possession charge for the needle and heroin if he gives up the dealer?"

Shelldrake smiled. "We can indeed. Now, get him in the interview room, and I will sit in the observation area and watch as you work your magic. Just remember, probie, never promise, only offer that we may be able to get the felony dropped. All depends on what we get as a result of the intel we get from him. He also needs to know that we will never divulge our sources, get it?"

Nikolai walked in the back where the detainee was sitting in his cell, then walked him into a nearby interview room. Nikolai put the squeeze on the man, letting him know that he was about to go down for possession of the heroin.

He also explained to the prisoner that if he cooperated by providing who the dealer was and where that dealer could be located, if it turned into something worthwhile, the possession charges could be eliminated. In other words, two felonies could be removed.

It took a little bit of time, but just as Nikolai attempted to walk out of the interview room, the defendant opened up and laid out all of the details regarding the dealer, his whereabouts and so forth. Nikolai in turn assured the prisoner he would go to work on this and let him know over the next day or so, before arraignment. He locked the prisoner into a cell and asked the jailer to keep an eye on the suspect as he could end up having withdrawals.

Nikolai approached his training officer on the way out to the unit. "It's about 2015 hours. Boss, you up for the adventure I proposed earlier, seeing how we have all this good intel?"

"What the hell! Let's give it a go!" Shelldrake replied.

Nikolai drove to the south side of the District 4 slums and gang territory, home of HTF, a bunch of stoner gangsters trying to make a name for themselves, run by a hardcore little bastard named Ruben Prince. They were also home to the Shakin' Cats and San Fer gangs. Nikolai killed the lights, rolled down the windows, and flipped the switch that blocked the brake lights from lighting up. Watching, listening, sneaking around in the dark, Nikolai stopped the unit in the 600 block of Kalisher St. and suggested they walk a foot patrol. Shelldrake agreed and told Nikolai, "Before we head out, switch over to frequency two and let dispatch know where we are and what we're doin' alright?" Nikolai did so, and the two headed out. As the two walked quietly though the residential neighborhood, slipping into the overgrown bushes that lined the front yards and driveways of the small homes there, one could hear what one would never hear driving a car around a neighborhood: TVs playing, people talking, an argument between spouses here and there.

Nikolai always creeped around late at night with his pals when he was a kid; he was always amazed at how clearly he could see once his eyes adjusted to the darkness. This was quite the same, except he wasn't creeping and capering; he was creeping to catch the caperer.

There was suddenly someone walking up behind them. The cops slid into the trees with a finger over their lips. Their radios were on, but they had earpieces in, so no one can hear them. The teenager, clad in black, walked by them briskly, not seeing either officer. Out of a dark driveway a short male Hispanic emerged. The two men chatted, and they heard the footbound pedestrian say, "I need a ten-dollar balloon."

The man who had emerged from the darkness looked around suspiciously, reached into his mouth, and removed a small balloon, exchanged it for a ten dollar bill, and the two split. The teenager walked back toward the direction he came from, and the dark figure that emerged from the driveway walked backward into the darkness.

Nikolai snuck toward the dealer, found him in the shadows, and gripped the suspect's wrist with one hand, placing him in a highly painful wrist lock while gripping the suspect's throat with the other.

Nikolai whispered, "LAPD, fuckstain, spit the dope out of your mouth." Seconds went by as the suspect briefly struggled. Nikolai whispered again, "Listen to me, spit the shit out, or so help me, the only thing that will beat you to the hospital is the headlights of the ambulance you are riding in, you pickin' up what I'm layin' down?"

The suspect looked out the corner of his eyes, which were rather large and in fear. Nikolai was looking around to make sure he didn't get outflanked. The suspect spat out seven small black balloons. Nikolai removed one hand from the suspect's throat, applied a little pressure to the suspect's wrists, and commanded the suspect to put his other hand on his head. He then simultaneously pulled that wrist around and behind the suspect's back and cuffed the wrist he had in a wrist restraint. Nikolai commanded in a whisper, "On your knees, quietly."

The suspect did as he was told. Nikolai put on a glove and picked up the seven black balloons, placing them in his pocket. He looked down the block where Shelldrake has the buyer cuffed.

Nikolai walked his suspect quietly toward his partner and was patting down the restrained drug dealer. To his surprise, he found a small .38 caliber revolver. He removed it and placed it in his back pocket. Nikolai reached for his radio to call dispatch.

Shelldrake laughed as he stuffed his prisoner into the backseat of the unit that was cleverly hidden in the alley nearby. "I got the balloon out of this kid's pocket, nothing else, what'd you get?"

Nikolai smiled as he stuffed the drug dealer in the back seat. "I hit the jackpot, Jefe, .38 revolver, and seven balloons of heroin." He removed the pistol and one of the balloons and proudly displayed them to his Field Training Officer.

They arrived at the station, closed the sally port gate, secured their weapons in the gun lockers, and removed the two prisoners from the unit. They escorted the two into the holding cells, leaving them cuffed for a bit, letting the jailer know they wanted to leave the detainees uncomfortable for a short time so they could try to get them loosened up enough to see what kind of information they could get out of them.

Shelldrake said, "Nikolai, get to work on the arrest report, and I will help out booking for the time being. We can tag team the evidence after the report is done."

Nikolai gave him a thumbs-up and got started on the IBM typewriter. Moments later, Shelldrake walked in. "Here's the name and DOB for the two upstanding citizens we have in custody and their booking numbers, kid."

Nikolai responded with a thank you and a smile, gleaming because he was trusted with writing the arrest report. This was what it's all about. Once he finished the arrest report, he noticed that the booking of the two was completed about the same time. The two men walked into the break room. They each got a cup of coffee, and Shelldrake read the arrest report.

Nikolai was sipping his coffee, trying not to act stressed. Shelldrake looked up, set the report down, and said, "Well shit, kid, I couldn't have done this better myself! Outfucking standing; let's get the evidence booked in and get our asses back in the field!"

They walked into the evidence prep room. The first step was removing the tar from the balloons and weighing them. Shelldrake placed each one into its own plastic bag, sealing them, then sliding them into the evidence envelope and documenting it on the form. Next up, the ten rounds of ammo that were in the suspect's pocket are one item, the bullets found in the .38 are the next, and then then the .38 revolver, its color, its serial number are documented. Nikolai bagged the bullets and labeled them. He then took the handgun, securing it in its own box with the cylinder out of the weapons frame and secured so when the box is opened, it will be obvious the weapon is rendered safe. All items documented, Nikolai ran to copy the evidence log itself and placed the original into the evidence locker, writing the number on the original form as well as the duplicate, then securing it. Shelldrake placed the entire file in the case folder and put it in the watch commander's mail slot for approval.

Shelldrake and Nikolai walked out back and got in the unit. Nikolai got on the radio. "The Double Deuce is on the loose, 10-8."

Dispatch responded, "Roger, 3-A-22 is 10-8."

Shelldrake grinned and said, "Get me to 776, kid, I need a cup of lifer's juice."

Nikolai sped off to the 7-11 at 776 N. Maclay as directed.

After they get out of the car, Shelldrake headed to the bathroom in the store's office—only the cops were allowed back there—and Nikolai poured them each a cup of coffee. Nikolai went up to pay and greeted the clerk, Raginder, with a big smile. Raginder was also from India. His family sent him to America to get a job, and he was working on a visa, while sending money home to help out his family. Our dollar was worth much more there than it is here. He told Nikolai that he slept on the couch of a two bedroom apartment shared with six others who work around the clock at the 7-11, also sending money home to their families.

Raginder made a motion of *no* when Nikolai tried to pay for the coffee. He put the cash on the counter anyway. Shelldrake walked out thanked Nikolai for the coffee and picked the cup off the counter.

They stood at the magazine counter at the front of the store which was part of the counter where the cash register was located. Shelldrake praises Nikolai. "Great work kid, the arrest report is clean, clear, and you wrote it fast! Now we're back in the field and can shag calls or find another body, whatever we decide. Let's see if the Sergeant requires any corrections before end of watch."

Nikolai and Shelldrake were standing at the counter between the magazine rack and the massive plate glass window at the front of the 7-11. A car was pulling into the parking spot right where they happen to be standing. It was getting closer, closer, closer when Nikolai noticed the car slow. Then all of a sudden the car roared and drove right through the plate glass window! Nikolai shoved Shelldrake out of harm's way and leaped over the counter behind Raginder screaming, "Get the hell outta the way!" landing on a mop bucket full of filthy water.

The car came to a rest, and Nikolai got up, literally covered with filthy water and a disgusted look on his face. He walked around the counter, opened the driver's door, put the Buick in Park and shut the car off. Shelldrake managed to get himself up, propping himself on the passenger fender of the car. Raginder had a *holy shit* surprised look on his face, and yelled with his Indian accent, "What the fuck are you doing, you turned my store into a God Damned Drive Thru!"

Nikolai had the driver exit the vehicle. He was an elderly man, at least eighty-five years of age. He was wearing an old velour burgundy running suit with white stripes running from the shoulders down the length of his arms and the same stripes running down the length of the pants. The driver was wearing bifocals that had to be two inches thick. The outfit and white shoes honestly looked like something one would wear in a 70s porn movie! If he weren't soaked in filthy water and pissed at having to leap to safety, Nikolai might be laughing his ass off.

"Are you alright, officer? My foot must have slipped off the brake and onto the accelerator, I am terribly sorry!" the man said apologetically.

Nikolai gained his composure, grabbed his handheld radio, and called dispatch. "22, can I get a rescue ambulance at my location. We have an 80-ish year old male who just converted 776 into a drive through liquor store. I am gonna need Budget Boardup and Black and White Tow as well."

Shelldrake looked at the old man for a moment and pulled Nikolai to the side. "Do you know who that old man is?"

With a disgusted look on his face, Nikolai said, "No, but I am sure you are gonna tell me."

Shelldrake whispered, "That's Mayor Martinez, well, he was mayor about twenty years ago, I think."

Nikolai laughed. "Well, let's find out. Sir, do you have your license, registration, and proof of insurance with you, please?"

The man removed his wallet from his pocket and

politely informed Nikolai that the registration and insurance were in the glove box. Nikolai retrieved the paperwork, and sure enough, it was former Mayor Martinez. Trouble is, the former mayor had a glove box full of prescription narcotics and was higher than a kite on what appeared to be opiates. Nikolai looked at Shelldrake. "Well, I'm either gonna book him or write him, your choice, boss?"

Shelldrake grinned and patted Nikolai on the shoulder. "It's your call, stud. Either way you go, you're gonna catch hell, but ya gotta do somethin."

The ticket book came out, the citation written, family members were called, and the ambulance arrived to check the mayor out.

Nikolai wrote the paper, Shelldrake took the statement from Raginder just as the tow truck arrived. The mayor was given a clean bill of health, just high as a kite, just as his daughter arrived.

She approached Shelldrake. "Is he okay?"

Shelldrake responded, "He is very lucky, young lady."

"What are you going to do with his car?" she asked.

Shelldrake bowed his head, frowned a bit, tried not to laugh, and pointed at Nikolai, who was having the mayor sign the citation. "He's your man, he can explain it to you."

She walked over, hugged her father. "You okay, Dad?" she said sympathetically.

He growled, "I'm fine, but I damn near killed these three!"

She introduced herself as Lizzy Martinez and looked at Nikolai and asked what happened. Nikolai, still covered in muck and soaked, sighed and said, "Well, miss, your dad's foot apparently slipped off the brake pedal, and he accelerated, driving the car into the window as you can see, forcing us to duck and cover. We're just glad everyone is okay, especially him."

"What happens next?" Lizzy asked.

Nikolai cleared his throat and looked at Shelldrake who had to turn away trying not to laugh.

"Well, ma'am, I have impounded the car, and I have written your father a citation, and I am confiscating his license for further re-evaluation."

Lizzy looked at him. "What does that mean?"

Nikolai was obviously frustrated and said, "Well, ma'am, I am sending the license to DMV and requesting an evaluation of your father be conducted to determine if he should be driving or not, this is pretty serious, and he could have killed someone."

"I see," she said. She escorted her father to the passenger side of her car and sat him down, closing the door behind him. She walked back over the Nikolai and asked, "Do you think you could just write the ticket rather than taking his license? I will keep him out from behind the wheel of any car, I promise."

Nikolai politely informed her, "No ma'am, due to

the severity of this situation, protocol dictates that we proceed in this fashion, I am sorry."

Nikolai handed the ticket to Lizzy and informed her where the car would be held. She tore the ticket from his hand and returned to her vehicle briskly and scowled at the officers as she proceeded off.

When the board up company showed up, Nikolai pulled a report number for the incident and gave all the information to Raginder so he could report this incident to the driver's insurance company and get the ball rolling to repair the shop.

Nikolai collected the six bottles of pills, and the two men headed to the station. They wrote the traffic collision report, Nikolai booked the pills into evidence and counted out every pill and confirmed what they were by using the PDR, or the *Physicians' Desk Reference*. As they were doing so, the Sergeant walked into the report room, "You guys are just shit magnets, ya know that, right?"

Shelldrake laughed and responded, "What the hell are you talking about, Sarge?"

The Sergeant snarled. "You two idiots impounded the mayor's car, that's what! For fuck's sake! You also came up with the brilliant move to paper fuck the poor man and pull his license for re-evaluation? Shit, and you two are booking pills into evidence! The Chief is gonna have your nuts in a sling come Monday, you know that, right?"

Nikolai commented, "Former mayor, Sarge, not mayor."

Sergeant Brown snarled again and snapped, "Well Nikolai, the guy who decided to make Belknap Chief of Police twenty years ago. I am certain the Chief is gonna see him as the mayor when the shit hits the fan on Monday. You gonna need overtime to wrap this shit show up?"

Shelldrake smiled. "Negative, sir, we're all done here."

The Sergeant rubbed his hand through his hair. "Then get the hell outta here, will ya. I am gonna get my stripes fed to me for letting you idiots do this to the mayor, I just know it," Sergeant Brown said, mumbling as he walked away.

Nikolai was supposed to go out to meet everyone at the Palomino Station this evening. Lord knows he hadn't seen any of them in over six months. Janette was certainly going to be upset that he wasn't going to be there. Before Nikolai left the station, he called Janette's home number and left a voice message that he got hung up at work late. Better than nothing they say. Nikolai headed home.

CHAPTER
TWELVE

Nikolai slept in. It was, after all, Sunday! He got home at two a.m. and managed to go right to sleep. Waking up at ten gave him eight hours, which felt like a lifetime. He poured a cup of coffee and managed to catch his roommate Jake at home. They sat around drinking coffee and discussed Jake's desire to move in with his girlfriend, abandoning the rental they had shared for quite some time. Nikolai made them both eggs and bacon, and the conversation went well as the two needed to move on. One to end the ridiculous commute and the other, well, so he could start a life with a woman who Nikolai thought was the spawn of Satan. The discussion ended with them agreeing to work together as they found other living accommodations.

Jake thanked Nikolai for breakfast and headed off to see his girl. Jake got in the shower and decided to head into the station to get a workout in. He arrived at the station around one p.m. and decided to do some shoulders, then run a couple of miles and work legs and abs at the end, then do some studying before shift started at 3:45. Halfway through the work out, he heard the intercom buzz. "Drew, see the desk, Drew, see the desk."

Nikolai walked down the hall and stuck his head through the door, "Whadda ya need, brother?"

Dispatcher Hough smiled. "L-50 is here. He's been here for a few hours, just a heads up, I think he's gonna want a word with you."

Nikolai was a bit puzzled. "Any idea what about?"

The dispatcher simply shrugged. "He was asking about you earlier is all, thought I'd let you know."

Nikolai went back into the gym and finished his first volley of his workout and was about to take a break from the weights to run. As he made his way to the side door of the station house, the intercom buzzed again. "Drew to L-50's office. Drew to L-50's office."

Well shit, that wasn't the dispatcher, that was the Chief himself and he didn't sound happy, he thought.

Nikolai walked down the long corridor to the Chief's office. There was no one there, no lights on, just the light into the man's office. He stuck his head in, "Hey Chief, I need a shower, shall I clean up and come back in, sir?"

He got up from his desk and said, "No, come on over and have a seat, close the door will ya, kid."

Nikolai did as he was asked, and they sat on the casual leather couches that rested in front of the Chief's desk. The Chief stuck out his hand and shook Nikolai's and motioned for him to sit.

The Chief began, "How are you doin', son? Are you suffering from any post traumatic stress after the shooting?"

Nikolai responded, "No sir, I feel great and am still seeing the therapist once every two weeks now."

Chief Belknap responded, "Good, that's good, son. Look, I'm gonna cut to the chase. I wanna talk to you about Mayor Martinez. Since last night and into today, I have had my ass handed to me by that little shit ass daughter of his. She doesn't like you at all, by the way, but that isn't the problem."

Nikolai leaned forward with a concerned look on his face. "What is the problem, sir?"

The Chief leaned back on the couch with his hands folded in front of him and he said, "Well son, that man promoted me to chief twenty some years ago. He could have picked some others, trust me, there were some other qualified candidates out there. Some might even say, better suited for the job than I was, but he chose me. Now look, I am not asking you to shirk your duty, if you feel that you can't let this thing go and you need to use the full weight and measure you handed out on this thing, I will support you fully."

Nikolai leaned forward. "Well Chief, I was light on him sir. I could have booked him for DUI Opiates, sir, but just wrote him the ticket. I figured he didn't mean to drive in that condition, and I didn't want to be a total jerk, seeing how this thing happened on private property and no one was hurt and all."

Chief squinted his eyes, thought pensively for a moment. "Well alright then, you're taking a stand. I respect that, and I for one appreciate you being lenient on this thing."

He began to stand, and Nikolai spoke again. "Well, Chief, can I just release the man's vehicle, squash the ticket, and return his license to him?"

The Chief sat back down. "No, Nikolai, you can't, but I can, if those are your wishes. If you want to do that, you just say so, and I will handle all that for you, but it's your call, son. Just don't feel like you are being bullied into anything."

Nikolai thought about it for a moment. "Alright, Chief, let's call it a day and let the man go about his business."

The two men stood up, and the Chief patted him on the shoulder. "You're a good man Nikolai. I will pass that along to him and his daughter. I appreciate you doing this, and I will owe you one, son."

In Nikolai's head, he felt that the Chief had already done him a favor by first hiring him, and second, for not permanently benching him for the shooting. He thought to himself that by giving the former mayor a break, it would save the Chief some dignity.

Nikolai turned around and began to walk out of the office and stopped. He turned and looked at the Chief. "I see the difference between the letter of the law and the spirit of the law, Chief. In all honesty, I may have taken the accident a little personal last night. I am sorry you had to deal with this. Thank you for the talk and for your understanding."

Nikolai went back to the workout and finished up his rigorous chest and abdominal portion of the routine and decided it was time for a little cardio mixed in with some handgun training, He went to his locker, retrieved his hand gun, set it and two magazines on the bench and placed a target twenty feet away and secured the range. Getting the heart rate up, running right into the shooting range, and firing a couple clips to check his accuracy under stress prepares one for the worst. Nikolai hit the street, ran the three-mile circuit averaging a seven-minute mile for the first two, and kicked up the last mile to six minutes to get his heart pounding. He punched in the security code to get into the back parking lot of the station, did the same at the back door, and ran into the range where his Sig Sauer P-220 was waiting.

The gun held seven rounds in the magazine and

one in the chamber. He aimed, fired seven rounds, switched to his left hand, dropped the magazine, and reloaded and fired seven more, always careful to leave one in the chamber, counting the rounds as he fired. Switching hands was something he learned from his father; the thought was that if one's right arm was injured, being proficient with both hands was always smart.

He returned to the target so he could view it and was surprised by the accuracy of the grouping. He was dead center, and most of the center mass of the target was obliterated. He policed the area, took the weapon back to his locker, and secured it and went about the remaining portion of his workout, a brutal assault on the triceps and remaining two hundred reps of abdominals.

He went to the locker room, removed his cleaning equipment and handgun from his locker, and made a protein shake. Some of the guys were in the locker room and made fun of his protein drink and gun cleaning. He laughed and walked out and back down to the gun range.

He took his time disassembling the weapon and sipped the elixir of protein. Within thirty minutes, the weapon was cleaned, lubed, and ready for duty. He walked the unloaded weapon back to the locker room and stowed the weapon and gun cleaning gear. Nikolai took a quick shower, suited up, and then he went to dispatch and picked up a copy of the last two shift logs to see what had been happening in the city since he left. Not much, just some report calls, vehicle burglaries, reports of group fights at two of the parks, nothing mind blowing on the surface.

He filled his coffee cup, returned the daily log to dispatch, and decided to take a stroll around the city for some recon work. He walked out back, put on a black jacket and fired up the '69. He pulled out of the parking lot and drove around to the south end of the city off of Kalisher where the local gangs hang out and over to Las Palmas park, a known hangout for Shakin Cats, a local gang named after the group the stray cats who wore pompadours and leather jackets. Along Kalisher at Mott, there was new graffiti with an exed out name. Rival gangs use this to make other gangs aware that someone is about to get shot up or taken out.

Ruben Castro known as "El Mero Mero" was a fourteen-year-old ringleader of the gang known as High Times Familia. He had sprayed his elaborate moniker on the wall, and it had been crossed out. This was in Shakin' Cat territory and not to be taken lightly. Nikolai had something to play with during the shift, as long as his FTO was game.

Nikolai got back to the station. His mind was swimming with ideas as he gathered his gear and waited for Shelldrake to arrive. Sitting in the squad room in the back row, Nikolai penciled out a plan of action for the day. He wanted to have his thoughts clear for his training officer when he arrived. Shelldrake walked in the room, set his gear on the table, and headed to the break room, presumably to get a cup of coffee.

When Shelldrake returned with the daily log and sipped his coffee. Nikolai let him get into the game, figuring he'd wait for the corporal to speak first. The rest of the patrol gang, their dispatcher, and the patrol Sergeant started making their way into the room. Shelldrake returned the daily log to the Sergeant and sat back down. He went over the activity of the last two shifts since they had been there last. There was nothing heavy to report, and he mentioned as always the shift expectation for two greenies for the shift (meaning two tickets), assigned the units for the shift, and dismissed everyone.

Nikolai picked up all of the gear and posse box, and Shelldrake selected a shotgun from the armory as well as ammunition. They loaded up the car, and Shelldrake suggested that Nikolai drive the first half of the shift.

Nikolai loved driving. He just kept his enthusiasm to himself. Nikolai picked up the microphone and gave the typical 10-8 (in service), and dispatch responded, "Roger 1-A-22 is 10-8."

Nikolai drove to 146 Hubbard so Shelldrake could get his favorite cup of coffee, then they got out of the unit and walked into the store. Shelldrake got his coffee and made it the way he liked it, just one sugar, stirred it up as he looked around surveying the area, in and out. Nikolai was covering, looking around as a customer or two walked in, bought their desired items, and walked out after paying. He and Shelldrake made their way out to the unit. Shelldrake placed his foot onto the push bar and sipped his coffee. He looked at Nikolai and finally began chatting. "Well, probie, it's a quiet damn day, typical Sunday. Did you catch any fallout when you got in the station today?"

Nikolai thought for a moment. "I got in early and heard that the Chief was in and asking about me."

Shelldrake grinned as he was looking around sipping coffee. "The old man in on a Sunday, well shit, that isn't good!"

Nikolai said, "Oh yeah, it gets better, he called me into his office."

Shelldrake looked over the brim of his coffee cup. "Oh, how did the old man treat you?"

Nikolai smiled. "He was great, told me about his history with the mayor and would prefer that I didn't go forward with the shit storm I started."

Shelldrake laughed. "Oh, I have no doubt, I bet he gave you the letter of the law versus the spirit of the law crap, yes?"

Nikolai paused. "No, not at all. In fact, told me that he would prefer I not take the thing any further, but mentioned that there was absolutely no pressure, just wanted me to be lenient. I told the Chief that I was lenient, I could have arrested the mayor for DUI

Opiates and didn't. Chief said, 'Okay, then you're taking a stand, I respect your position,' got up and went back to his desk to sit down. I turned and got to his door and stopped, turned and told the Chief that I was struggling with my decision since last night. I also told him that I got the whole letter of the law versus spirit of the law thing and asked him how I could reverse what I had done. He told me that if that was what I wanted to do, he would handle it for me.

"He made it clear that it had to be my decision and that I had to understand, he wasn't asking me to make that choice. So, I told him that was my decision and asked him to take care of it. That was the end of it."

Shelldrake took another sip of his coffee and asked, "Well, how did that make you feel, letting the guy go, who damn near ran us over?"

Nikolai thought it over. "Rubbed me the wrong way. I would have let him go through the process. He may not be so lucky next time. But I also realize this, the incident did occur on private property, so, given all the facts, I am certain the man's daughter won't be letting him drive again. All I did by reversing the decision was really save a man's dignity."

Shelldrake smiled again. "So, you made peace with it. Good, in my opinion, you did the right thing. So, what do you have in mind for tonight? Any other politicians you want to piss off?"

Nikolai brought out his piece of paper and

mentioned what he saw driving around in his car before shift. "I thought we could harass some dirtbags tonight and see what pops up. Ultimately sir, I would love to get some dope or guns off one of these guys, but honestly, getting Castro off the street for a felony would be awesome."

Shelldrake nodded. "Dirtbags it is, lead the way, probie."

They mounted up and drove down to the area where Nikolai had found the graffiti and drove around the area blacked out (no lights or taillights). The streets were deathly quiet, like a ghost town. Around five a.m. they made their way to the southernmost part of town at the intersection of Sepulveda at Mission Boulevards, when a car exited the freeway breaking traction and sped northbound on Mission.

Shelldrake and Nikolai looked at one another in disbelief, and Nikolai hit the accelerator, simultaneously fastening his seatbelt, in an attempt to catch the vehicle. Shelldrake reached for the radio as if to put out a radio broadcast, but had no idea what kind of car they were chasing, what model it was, or even a color and realized that the car had literally vanished!

Nikolai made a quick right onto Mott and hit Maclay Street. Once at the corner, they looked both directions and caught the glimpse of taillights turning westbound on 1st Street right by the police station. They followed, and by the time they got to 1st Street, they saw the vehicle, a black Mustang, enter the police station parking lot. Nikolai followed in and got his push bars right on top of the rear bumper of the car and hit the red and blue emergency lights. He got on the PA system. "Okay, fucker, get your hands where I can see 'em!" The driver, off-duty reserve officer Sully, raised his hands out the window and slowly lowered all of his fingers except the two middle ones! The 1986 Black Ford Mustang was one of those that had a reputation for being extremely light and extremely fast.

Nikolai turned off the emergency lights, and Sully walked up laughing, "I knew I would have you chasin' me, thought you would have caught up faster than that!"

Shelldrake turned on his flashlight illuminating Sully's smiling face. "Nice job, dickhead, why are you in so early?"

Sully covered his eyes so he wasn't blinded by the flashlight. "I have court in the morning so thought I would take a quick nap, hit the gym, and shower up rather than trying to sleep in like a human. See you two fucktards in a couple hours."

Nikolai put the cruiser in Reverse and as he looked over his shoulder told Shelldrake, "There is something seriously not right about that guy!"

Shelldrake laughed. "Well, there is something not right with all of us, my friend!"

Nikolai parked the cruiser in a spot adjacent to

Sully and told Shelldrake he had to use the head and would be right back. He exited the police cruiser and headed toward the back door of the police station and observed that Sully's trunk looked like a transient had taken up residence there. In just a quick glance, he saw a lot of weird stuff, including a gray leather bag that had some sort of fastener at one end, Nikolai discarded it as a workout bag.

Nikolai used the urinal, washed his hands, and ran into Sully walking in the back door of the station as he was walking back out. They fist bumped as they walked by one another, and Nikolai made it back to the running patrol car. Nikolai got in the unit and backed out of the parking space and headed back to the area of Sepulveda and Mission to look for scoundrels and dirtbags lurking. The remainder of the shift was winding down, so Nikolai engaged in finding some traffic violators on their way to work. It was now about 6:30 a.m. so they just sat along the curb of Rinaldi facing westbound looking at the vehicles down both sides of Sepulveda.

Suddenly, Nikolai put the car in Drive and began to lurch into traffic. Shelldrake laughed and asked, "What did you see kid?"

Nikolai snuck between cars and pointed out a blue Nissan Sentra four door. "Check her out, Shell, she's putting on makeup with both hands, her visor is down, and she's obviously using her knees to steer the car!"

Shelldrake laughed out loud. "And I thought I had seen it all. Good goin', Nancy Drew!" Shelldrake picked up the mic and radioed it in. Shelldrake had the overhead lights on and hit a quick blast of the siren, and the vehicle pulled over. Nikolai parked the unit, strategically placing the passenger headlight of his unit behind the driver side tail light of the vehicle, in order to create a safe area for him to walk. They both exited the vehicle quickly as Nikolai placed it in Park. Shelldrake actually got out before the unit stopped fully. Nikolai approached the driver and gave his canned introduction. "Good morning, ma'am. I'm Officer Drew. May I see your license, registration, and proof of insurance please?"

The woman put her mascara brush down and began fumbling through her purse; Shelldrake is watching her through the passenger window. She found the items requested, and as she handed them to Nikolai, she asked, "May I ask what you are stopping me for, officer?"

Nikolai responded politely. "Absolutely, ma'am, for unsafe speed. You don't happen to have any outstanding warrants, do you ma'am?"

The woman's voice became irate. "No! I don't have warrants! Unsafe speed? I was barely doing ten miles per hour!"

Nikolai smiles. "Well I am glad you don't have warrants, ma'am. I will be back in a moment." The woman, a Hispanic female, about 5'1", weighing in at about 145, exited the vehicle and briskly walked after Nikolai, chastising him.

"Are you fucking kidding me, you have nothing better to do that harass working people with some lame speed thing?"

Shelldrake got between the woman and Nikolai who had turned around to face the woman now walking backwards.

Shelldrake asked the woman, "Ma'am, please get back in your vehicle. It's not the safest place to be out here with all the traffic."

The furious motorist was now yelling, arms flailing in the air. "Not until you tell me how the hell you think you can justify pulling me over for speeding when I was clearly doing ten miles per hour!"

Shelldrake cracks a grin. "Well, ma'am, the truth of the matter is that there is no safe speed while you have no hands on the steering wheel as you apply makeup with your visor down in such a fashion that you can barely see the car in front of you; ma'am, you nearly collided with the car in front of you three times while we were watching your automotive gymnastics."

Completely flabbergasted, the woman stopped speaking, her mouth open, jaw dropped. After a few moments, she yelled, "You have absolutely got to be fucking kidding me! If you two idiots actually have the unmitigated gall to write me a ticket for this shit, I am going to file a complaint with city hall, your chief, and anyone else who will listen."

Meanwhile Nikolai had already written the citation, had run her for warrants, and in discovering that she had no warrants, joined her at the passenger side hood of the unit.

Nikolai rested the citation book on the hood and gave his closing speech. "Ma'am, as I mentioned, I am citing you for unsafe speed for conditions, noting the facts mentioned to you by Officer Shelldrake. You are correct you have no warrants, and your license status is valid; now, if you will simply sign the bottom of the citation where the red X is, understanding, this is a promise to appear, not an admission of guilt, on or before the date shown below, you may be on your way!"

The tiny assailant and violator of traffic laws crosses her arms and said indignantly, "I am not signing this ticket," and started to walk away.

Shelldrake gets between her and her vehicle and pleads, "Now, ma'am, two things, we have all of your documentation. You don't want to leave that behind, and if you refuse to sign the citation, which as Officer Drew mentioned is NOT an admission of guilt, just a promise to appear in court, we will be forced to arrest you and store your vehicle, and that is going to absolutely ruin your day."

The woman stopped, turned around, and walked back to the waiting Officer Drew and ripped the pen from his hand. "I'm going to sign this, but you can count on seeing me in court, Officers!"

Nikolai removed the citation from the booklet, removed her copy for her, and gave her back her information as well as the citation and said, "Please be safe getting back into your vehicle, and please drive safe, ma'am."

She got back into her vehicle while Nikolai and Shelldrake continued to stand at the curb making certain she safely got on her way, and just as she pulled out, a hand pops above the roof line with her middle finger. When they entered their vehicle, Shelldrake put out over the radio "1-A-22 is 10-8 en route 10-19 EOW."

Dispatch acknowledged, "Roger 1-A-22, clear from traffic."

The time was now 0730 hours. Nikolai pulled the unit into the city yard and started pumping gas into the unit and filling out the daily patrol log. He topped off the tank and handed the posse box to Shelldrake so he could approve the notes while Nikolai drove them to the station. When they arrived, he parked the unit and made sure it was clean and stocked up with emergency supplies for the next shift.

They removed their uniforms and stored their gear, returning to their civilian clothing, and parted ways. As Nikolai made his way to the parking lot, there was a blast over the intercom. "Drew to the Chief's office." He stopped dead in his tracks, dropped his head dramatically, turned around, and headed down the hall.

———

Nikolai popped his head into the Chiefs office. "Yes sir," he says.

The Chief motioned him into the office. "Close the door please and have a seat!" He explained to Nikolai that it appeared the family of the suspect killed during the shooting was suing the department and Nikolai, as was the passenger that was hit by the stray bullet. "Don't be concerned. This will likely go on for some time, but there is no wrongdoing. The debate will be to let them run with the court case or have the city offer a settlement deal. Really comes down to whether or not the mayor, council, and city administrator feel that it's cheaper for the city to settle than to drag it out in court. I will keep you posted so you are not surprised or blindsided by a subpoena to appear."

Nikolai was sheet-white, and the Chief could tell he was stressed. "Look kid, I know it's scary, it's a new experience. Believe me son, we have your back in this, you're going to be fine."

CHAPTER
THIRTEEN

During the long drive home, Nikolai contemplated the possibility of being dragged through having to tell the story of this damned shooting all over again! The roar of the engine made by the '69 El Camino and the songs playing over the cassette player helped Nikolai leave the situation at work. After all, there was nothing he could do about it. He then pondered Sully's idiotic behavior this morning. Although, it wasn't the first time one of these guys did something to try to get one of the patrol dogs' goat, knowing how badly every cop wants to be involved in a high speed pursuit.

Nikolai arrived home at 9:30 a.m., took a shower, brushed his teeth, flossed, and went to bed. Six hours later at 3:30, he awoke on his own. Getting out of bed, he combined frozen fruit, some yogurt, and protein and made a protein shake. He took out his daytimer and looked at his to-do list for the day. It was time to mow the lawn, check the laundry, and wash the car. He started the load of laundry and let it run while he edged and mowed the front and rear lawns.

Then he assessed the El Camino for washing. It didn't really need a full wash, so he cleaned the windows, Centerline racing wheels, vacuumed the car out, and went inside to fold the laundry. In between all this, he made his patrol to-do list, the areas he planned to check in his beat and made a note to swing into the Detective Bureau to see if there was anything they needed him to do. These guys mostly ignored him, but there were a couple of detectives who appreciated that he was always trying to make their jobs easier.

The door leading into the kitchen from the garage popped open, and in walked Diamond Dave Shankland. He was one of Nikolai's oldest friends, going back to junior high school. Dave's mother hated Nikolai; she always thought that he was a bad influence on her son. He was always in trouble for ditching school, shoplifting, sneaking out of the house after the parents went to bed, the list went on. Whenever he got caught, he would blame Nikolai in order to divert the blame off himself. Dave was 5'9", built well, with rounded shoulders, probably from all the years of his mother brow beating him. What he lacked in stature, he made up in attitude—the guy could make a bunch of bodies in the morgue sit up and laugh. "What the fuck is goin' on, man, I heard you are about to lose your roommates?"

Nikolai stood up and grabbed Dave by the hand and pulled him in for a hug. "That's right, so I think I'm gonna move to LA. This drive is killin' me, brotha!"

Dave got a big shit-eating grin on his face. "Well, hell, man, count me in. I need a change of scenery! I gotta seriously get out of the Inland Empire and honestly, outta my damn parents' house!"

Nikolai smiled. "Brother, you work at your dad's gas station in Corona. You are not gonna want to make that drive back and forth the valley every day. Trust me, I hate it!"

Dave again smiles. "Niki, I have enough money saved that I don't have to work for a year, I can afford the deposit and rent, and I will find work out there, don't you worry. I am sick of workin' for my dad and living under their roof. When do we start looking for a place?" They agreed they would research rentals and go out over Diamond Dave's day off, in two days.

Nikolai put on his workout gear: bright colored parachute pants and a matching baggy shirt that made him look like he just stepped out of a MC Hammer music video. He secured the house and headed in to work. He wanted to arrive early enough so he could stop into the Detective Bureau before everyone left. He walked in and caught Detective Bedo sitting at the homicide desk. Bedo smoked like a chimney. Damned good investigator though and always treated Nikolai like he was of value, not just a punk rookie.

"Hey, Detective, what's shakin' today, anyone or anything you are lookin' for or need me to stir up for you?" Nikolai asked. The detective stood up and stretched, then put his arm around Nikolai's shoulder and escorted him out the door into the detective parking lot.

"Come on, kid, let's take a ride, I need a Coke!" Bedo lit a cigarette, and the two men squeezed into the Ford LTD 2. The damn car felt like a coffin to the two large men, you couldn't squeeze a slip of paper between them. Bedo drove to 146 Hubbard, the 7-11 store that everyone loved. Bedo got a Super Big Gulp, filled it 1/4 of the way with ice, the rest with Coke.

Bedo looked intensely at Nikolai and began, "Kid, this god damned Gentleman Bank Robber has me baffled. He is in and out and never makes any damned mistakes. I wish I had something else to have you put your sights on, but I don't. I know you don't take naps out there, so while you are drivin' around, shake down everyone and see if anyone knows anything about this dirtbag for me. I know it's a long shot, but one never knows what you might come up with."

Nikolai laughed. "Happy to do whatever I can, I'll shake down everyone single low crawling douche bag until we catch the fucker."

Bedo tried to pay for the soda, but the clerk

refused the money. As Bedo turned to walk away, he left a dollar bill on the counter anyway. As they drove back to the station Bedo asked, "When are you gonna move out this way, kid? That drive is gonna kill you one way or another, I am tellin ya." Nikolai joyfully responded, "In a couple of days my buddy and I are gonna look for a place to rent out this way. My roommate gave thirty days notice the other day, so I need to get a move on."

Bedo smiled and patted him on the back. "That's excellent. I have a pal who owns rentals all over. When we get back to the station, I'll give you his number. He's a cop too."

They got back to the station and Bedo pulled out his notebook and wrote down the name and number of the cop who had rental properties and handed it to Nikolai, then drove off.

Nikolai went into the gym, cranked up the music, and began the assault on his workout of the day. After he was done, he showered up, suited up, and got ready for roll call. The midnight hour was rapidly approaching, and it was time to get his unit set up the way his training officer liked it. Shelldrake spoke up at the end of roll call and told the shift Sergeant that he wanted to send Nikolai out as an L-Unit—a one man car. Shelldrake went on to say that he thought it was about time for the rookie to go out on his own and that he would ghost him, meaning he would follow along and keep an eye on the rookie. The

Sergeant agreed and assigned Nikolai to L-27, and Shelldrake would be designated as X Ray 1.

Nikolai walked out with Shelldrake, and the training officer told him to simply do what he's been taught and call out if he needed assistance. They parted company, and Nikolai went to work setting up the unit his way; which surprisingly was just like Shelldrake liked it! He got the unit ready and reached for the microphone and broadcasted proudly, "1-L-27 is 10-8"! He pulled out of the parking lot, and a sense of pride overtook him. *This is what it's all about,* he thought.

He pulled out onto 1st Street and turned right and then left onto Maclay and headed to the ghetto. Over the radio he heard the dispatcher. "1-L-27."

He responded, "27 go ahead."

"1-L-27, respond to 465 Jackman Street, reporting party just returned home to an open door, possible burglary in progress, X Ray 1, respond to back."

Nikolai immediately responded, and Shelldrake responded right after. "X Ray 1 enroute, 1 minute ETA."

Nikolai arrived in the area and turned out all of the unit's lights and parked two houses down. He shut off the unit and broadcast that he was on the scene. Shelldrake arrived at the same time. They walked slowly and methodically toward the home and were approached by a middle-aged Hispanic woman who spoke in Spanish letting them know she owned the home and was the person who called. Shelldrake told him that this was his handle; he was just there to watch.

Nikolai addressed the woman in Spanish, and asked the woman what she saw. She informed him that she had been out with friends, and when she got home she saw her front door open and the lights were on, but there was no movement. Nikolai asked if there was anyone else in the home or any dogs they should be aware of. She said she lived alone.

"How many bedrooms and bathrooms are there in the home, ma'am?" he asked.

She said that there was one bedroom and one bathroom to the left as they entered the house and two bedrooms and one more bathroom in the master bedroom just past the kitchen. As they were approaching the house, another unit arrived.

Officer Sorelson approached and asked what the situation was. Nikolai told him what he knew and requested that Sorelson cover the rear of the residence and told him there were no dogs to be concerned about. Nikolai was nervous, but also had a strange calmness to him. He looked at Shelldrake and asked him to cover him as they entered and cleared the residence. Shelldrake smiled, and said, "You got it, Nancy." They loved to call him Nancy like Nancy Drew, which ticked him off to no end. What the hell kind of nickname was that?

Fortunately for them, this was a single-story home

which made it easier to search and cover from the back. Sorelson carefully crouched down and walked to the back of the house as Nikolai and Shelldrake slowly entered the front door with guns drawn. As they walked down the hallway, Shelldrake had his weapon pointing over Nikolai's shoulder. They got to the family room and kitchen area, where Nikolai pointed he was going to the left and motioned that Shelldrake cover the uncleared areas. Nikolai cleared the bathroom and the bedroom, walked out, and gave a thumbs-up indicating the room was clear. He walked up to and past Shelldrake and carefully walked around the family room wall away from the wall and making sure not to let the gun go around the wall to alert anyone who may be lurking there! He approached Shelldrake with another thumbs-up. The two men slowly walked down the hall to the two remaining bedrooms. They cleared them both and observed that the master bedroom appeared to be ransacked and there was no garage, just a carport. Nikolai put out a Code 4, meaning the situation was under control, and let Sorelson know to meet them at the front.

Nikolai walked back out the front door to greet the homeowner, and as they walked through the front door, they noticed that it was unlocked and there were no pry marks. Nikolai asked the women to escort them through the home to see if anything was disturbed or missing. He also asked the woman if it was common for her to leave the front door unlocked. She told him that she almost always locked the door, but forgot from time to time. As they walked through the residence, the woman noticed nothing disturbed. Nikolai noted the master bedroom's condition, and she said that was pretty normal. She worked a lot and wasn't a very good housekeeper. He pulled Shelldrake aside and told him he felt that she had left the door unsecured and probably ajar and it appeared that there was no burglary. Shelldrake agreed. "I'm going to give her my card and let her know if she finds anything missing to call the station and ask for me so I can write a report, sound good sir?" he asked Shelldrake.

Shelldrake nodded. "Well done, kid."

As they walked away from the home, Shelldrake told Nikolai to meet him at 146 for a cup of coffee and a debriefing. Upon arrival, Nikolai saw Shelldrake sitting on the hood of his unit backed into its parking space near the wall on the north side of the convenience store. This was his favorite spot as it was secluded and didn't allow for anyone to sneak up on his backside. Nikolai backed his unit in next to Shelldrake, got out, and addressed the training officer. Shelldrake asked the rookie how the deployment of the last radio call went.

Nikolai had been thinking about it since the call terminated and said politely and with no ego "I thought it went well. We covered all angles of the building and the interior deployment went smoothly. There can always be corrections, Shell. I suppose the real moment of truth would have come if we would have discovered a suspect and things went bad."

The training officer thought for a moment with a stern look about his face, put his arm around Nikolai, and walked him in to the 7-11 and said, "Perfect response, you're right, it's all fun and games until the shit hits the fan; you know this, you handled it very well during your altercation. I have no doubt you will handle it just fine when and if it happens again!"

The two men stepped inside the convenience store and greeted the cashier. Today it was Mangot Singh. He was always so gracious and always greeted them with, "Hello buddy, how are you today!"

The shift was nearing its end; over the radio was a break in the silence. "Control to 1-L-27, 10-19 and see L-30," meaning that Nikolai was being summoned to the police station to see the shift sergeant. Nikolai got on the radio and replied "1-L-27 roger, be there in less than 5."

Nikolai arrived at the station and rather than emptying his unit, walked straight into the Sergeant's office. Sergeant Ramsley was a big corn-fed Okie, 6'4", about 250, and had hands so big, it made his Colt .45 caliber long slide handgun look like a miniature. They guys called him "Roger RamJet" for whatever reason. The man had a reputation for being a hell raiser back in his early days as a cop.

Shelldrake had told Nikolai a story that while working patrol in a '58 Chevy powered by a 409 (a notorious big block that Chevrolet built, known for having a lot of horse power and torque). A suspect refused to pull over for ole RamJet. So, Ramsley accelerated his unit until the push bars were on the bumper of the suspect's old Ford Fairlane and accelerated from 75 miles per hour to over 100 and backed off. This little maneuver scared the shit out of the suspect who immediately pulled the car over and put his hands out the driver's side window, surrendering to Ramsley. His voice was gruff and worldly as it should be given that the man was sixty years old and had served in the Marine Corps as a gunnery sergeant during World War II. Shelldrake was sitting in the room as well, and Ramsley asked him to take a seat.

———

The gruff Sergeant handed Nikolai a clipboard and told him to look over the evaluation written by Shelldrake. As he read it, Ramsley told him that Shelldrake felt he was performing at above average level for the time on the job and was recommending he move onto the next level of training. Ramsley told him that he was taking over as watch commander day shift in two days and was moving Nikolai to the same shift to begin working with Field Training Officer

Don Hardy. Nikolai signed the evaluation and thanked Shelldrake for the kind words. Ramsley mentioned that Hardy was a good solid cop, and was really tough on Officer Safety scenarios and report writing. He didn't suspect Nikolai was going to have any issues, but bumped the current Sergeant so he could be around to look over Nikolai's training. The men adjourned. Nikolai emptied his patrol unit, put away his gear and got into his civilian clothes.

Shelldrake walked him out to the parking lot and said, "Hey, kid, a few of us are heading over to The Corral on Osborne Street. It's a cop bar, and they serve a great breakfast for us. It's customary to get an invite when you pass phase two of training, call it a ritual, so we'll see ya there." Nikolai agreed and drove to the bar. He pulled into the dirt parking lot, and as he got out looked at his clean El Camino and shook his head in disgust knowing that not only was the exterior of the car now filthy, but he was going to have to completely scrub under the hood and wash down the undercarriage. The place was run down on the outside and dark as hell as he walked in the front door. He allowed his eyes to adjust and saw a group of men sitting at a large group of tables put together in the middle of the place. Shelldrake pulled him up a chair. All of the guys were busy talking and laughing, ten in all, including Sergeant Ramsley.

The waitress walked around and took his order, which was a cup of coffee, two eggs over easy, polish sausage, hash browns, and wheat toast. Shelldrake told her to bring the kid a Johnnie Walker Black on the rocks. Nikolai looked over at him. "Another tradition I take it?"

Shelldrake said, "Well hell yes, we are going to clink glasses to ya, kid and wish you well onto the next level!"

The waitress brought over several drinks as well as Nikolai's whiskey. Shelldrake stood and said, "Raise a glass, lads, to Nikolai Drew, one hell of a good cop. May he move onto the next level with great vigor, and may he enjoy a long and adventurous career with the LAPD. Salud!"

The others all followed with, "Salud!"

CHAPTER
FOURTEEN

T wo days off are something to look forward to, and Nikolai wasn't going to waste them. He absolutely loved having Mondays and Tuesdays off. Everyone was working, so the days were easy to navigate through. He just had to remember that he had to go back to work early Wednesday for day shift—that was going to make for a wicked commute. He drove back to the station and decided to call the cop that Bedo referred to him about a rental and get that ball rolling. Nikolai sat down in the report room and removed the piece of paper from his wallet. The name with a 310 number that belonged to Sergeant Francis Accord. He picked up the phone in the report room and called the number. Five rings and no answer; the message machine came on, and the relaxed male voice said, "Accord here, you know what to do, so do it!"

Nikolai said quickly, "Sergeant Accord, this is Nikolai Drew of LAPD Foothill Division, Detective Bedo gave me your number and said you may be able to help me with a rental here in the valley. Call my pager number when you get a moment, 909-867-5309, and I will call you back as soon as I can."

Nikolai decided to hit the gym for a workout and wait for a page from the wayward landlord in hopes he would return his call before he decided to head home. He suited up and decided to take a quick mile run to warm up, so he walked out the back door of that station and took his usual route down First Street then southbound on Brand to Third Street and headed east. Along the way he was singing cadence to keep his breathing regular. "I had a little girl in a Mississippi town, she said Marine Corps. life was bringin' her down. She said it was either her or the Corps. a well I won't be goin back to Mississippi no more, left right on your left right left, I said a left right left, a left riiiiiiight left." Within less than seven minutes he was back at the station, walked into the weight room, and began warming up on the incline bench press. Today was a chest and triceps day, and he always liked starting with the incline bench first as it was the toughest.

Forty-five minutes went by, and he was just finishing up the chest portion of the workout when his pager went off. It was a 213 area code number with an extension 66 at the end. Nikolai assumed that meant to call the number and ask for that extension. He made the call, and a secretary picked up. "LAPD Detective Bureau, can I help you?"

Nikolai said, "Yes, ma'am, Nikolai Drew, extension 66 please."

"Hold please, I will put you through to Sergeant Accord."

A loud deep voice came over the line. "Accord here." Nikolai told him the story that he had been given this number by Detective Bedo who said that he might be able to assist with a rental.

Accord got right to the point. "Yeah, Bedo told me you were a fire breather and that you'd be calling. Are you in the valley now, son?" Nikolai said he was. Accord told him to meet him at the Van Nuys Station in thirty minutes so they could meet and talk.

Nikolai got off the phone, went into the locker room and took a hobo's bath (washcloth soap and water to the pits and groin), put on some clothes, deodorant, and cologne and jetted off to Van Nuys to meet with the Sergeant.

After a short drive through surface streets and a short hop onto the 5 Freeway, Nikolai arrived at Van Nuys Station and parked in the employee parking lot. He walked into the lobby and asked the desk officer to let Sergeant Accord know he had a visitor and gave the desk officer his name. Shortly thereafter, the Sergeant opened the lobby door and called Nikolai's name. He stood and gave the Sergeant a nod acknowledging who he was, and the Sergeant motioned him in. Accord escorted Nikolai to his office, and they sat at the guest chairs together. Accord asked "So, I hear from Bedo you are a solid hard working and dedicated guy. He doesn't like many people, so I take that pretty seriously. What are you looking for?"

Nikolai replied thoughtfully, "My buddy Dave and I will be living together; we are long time friends. Neither one of us need a lot, and we aren't partiers either. A three bedroom with two bathrooms would be great, if you know of anything."

Accord smiled and stood up. "Let's go for a drive. I have one I want to show you; they are moving out in three weeks. I can probably walk you through if they aren't home." The two men walked out back of the station house and got into Accord's unmarked unit. "The house is in Devonshire Division. We call it Club Dev. because nothing ever goes down in that area. It's close to everything and a nice neighborhood."

Ten minutes later they arrived at the home. There were no cars in the driveway, so they walked up. It was a single-story house, plain, but clean. White paint, dark brown trim with shutters and a dark brown colored garage door and front door that matched the trim. Accord knocked on the door, and after a few moments with no one answering, he unlocked the door and escorted Nikolai into the home, smiling.

"The renters know I am showing you the home, so come on in fellas."

As they entered the foyer, it opened up into a spacious family room. There was no dining room, only a breakfast nook with seating at a center island. As they made their way down the hallway, they passed the common bathroom. It was large with two sinks and a nice walk-in shower with no tub. The two bedrooms that lined the hallway both cascaded down the right side of the home. Both bedrooms were oversized, twelve feet deep by fourteen feet in length, with large closets. At the far end of the hallway was a fourth door that opened up into the master bedroom which had its own bathroom. The two other bedrooms were quite a bit smaller, but this one appeared to be much bigger, fourteen foot by twenty, and it had a walk-in closet.

They walked back to the kitchen, and Nikolai noticed it had basic cabinets in oak with tan tiles for a countertop. The stove was ample with an oven and lots of storage. Toward the front of the house to the right, was a door that led to the two-car garage from inside the home. They walked in, it was lined with cabinets that were well put together for storage and a cut out at the back of the garage with a workbench and room for a roll-away tool box.

Accord escorted Nikolai out the side door of the garage into the back yard which was low maintenance. An entertainer's dream, it had a free standing, covered patio with a BBQ, bar, and stools. There was also a patio off the master bedroom of the house with plenty of room for seating. The rest of the yard was all pavers with some planters with palm trees but nothing that required any effort. The two men made their way back through the home, out the front door, and back to the street. Accord told Nikolai, "This was my wife's and my home for years. That's why it looks the way it does. The couple who rents it now are moving out of state, so I really want a solid renter to take it over. It sounds like you are my guy. I would like to talk with your current landlord if you don't mind."

Nikolai smiled. "What is the monthly rent, Sarge, I don't know if it's in our budget. It is way nicer than I expected."

Accord laughed. "Niki, my boy, how about $1,400.00 per month? The home is paid off, I just want a good tenant!"

Nikolai grinned. "Sarge, you have a deal, what do you need from us?"

Accord got into his car and as Nikolai got in said, "Let's head back to my office, and I will have you fill out the lease agreement and go from there. I won't even hassle you for deposit!"

When they returned to Van Nuys Station, Nikolai and Accord returned to office, and Nikolai filled out a lease document with all his and Diamond Dave's information naming Nikolai as the sole lessee and

Dave as the roommate. Before signing it, Nikolai paged Diamond Dave from Accord's office with a 911 at the end. Sergeant Accord left the happy new tenant in the office to wait for the returned call. Before the Sergeant could return, Diamond Dave called in.

Nikolai answered the phone, "Sergeant Accord's Desk!"

Dave asked, "Hey, Niki, is that you?"

Nikolai laughed. "Yeah, man, it's me. You are not gonna believe it. I got us a house in Northridge!" They talked back and forth, went over the cost for rent, and Dave told him to sign the agreement and lock it in. Moments later, Accord returned, and Nikolai handed him the signed application. The two men shook hands, and the date was set for the move in!

Nikolai left the Van Nuys Station with a spring in his step. He got in the El Camino, fired her up, and headed home. He was so excited, he didn't know if he could even get to sleep. He plugged in his favorite Ozzy Osborne tape, and as "Crazy Train" came on, he could feel the El Camino roar to life as he headed down the 5 South all the way to the 10 Freeway! Once heading east on the 10, he exited onto Hamner and headed south through Ontario and finally into Norco and turned left onto 6th Street. He made the drive into the back parts of Norco then into Riverside past the old Crestlawn Cemetery.

As he passed by there every time, he would say a prayer for his grandmother and grandfather who were buried there. Arlington intersected with La Sierra Avenue, and he turned right and fifteen minutes later, he made it home. Now thoroughly exhausted after being up for sixteen hours, Nikolai took advantage of the house being quiet. By the time his head hit the pillow, he was out cold.

CHAPTER
FIFTEEN

The weekend went by quickly, in Nikolai's case the weekend being Monday and Tuesday. Now it was back to work Wednesday! Getting up at 4:30 a.m. to start the journey back to LA was not Nikolai's idea of fun. He got his coffee and his protein shake and began the drive. An hour later he arrived at the station, now fully awake. He parked the El Camino, locked it up, and went in to secure his car keys and warm up for his run. The sun was just starting to come up as he rounded the last part of the three-mile track around the area surrounding the police station. He walked right into the weight room and began the ritual of training. Dayshift begins at 0800 hours, but roll call begins at 0745 hours. Nikolai had about an hour and a half to knock out the three-mile run and workout for the day. Managing the time correctly, he had plenty of time to shower and suit up!

He got out of the shower, suited up, and went straight in to dispatch so he could read the daily log and get a feel for what had been happening over his days off. He then walked back to the Detective Bureau to see what Bedo had for him. In truth, Nikolai felt attached to Bedo somehow, like the connection kept him up to speed with all of the goings on around the city. He felt it made him a better cop. The Detective Bureau was a ghost town, but the Detective Secretary was sitting at her desk getting ready for her day. Nikolai greeted her as usual, and just then, the big steel back door that led into the bureau office opened up and Bedo walked in. Nikolai approached Bedo and shook his hand. "Well, brother, that lead you hooked me up with on the rental paid off. We're moving in there in two weeks, so thank you!"

Bedo laughed. "Good things happen to good people, kid!"

Nikolai was all smiles and continued. "I have to tell you this whole two plus hour drive a day getting here and home is such a drag. I can't wait till I'm just ten minutes out! What's new with the bank robber, by the way, anything?"

Bedo motioned to Nikolai to follow him, and they walked down the hall past the Chief's office and into the break room. Bedo poured himself a cup of coffee, and Nikolai did the same. Bedo lowered his voice so no one but Nikolai could hear. "Kid, this fucker hit us again yesterday, made away with $25,000 in cash."

Nikolai was now frustrated and replied, "I have been watching all over for days. It's just a matter of time before one of us gets in the way of this son of a bitch. I want this guy bad, brother!"

Bedo patted Nikolai on the back. "Yeah, we all do, kid. Get to roll call, and we will chat later. Your new FTO should be an interesting experience for you. Good luck over the next week."

The two men parted ways, and Nikolai walked into the squad room and sat at the front table as expected of a rookie. Sergeant Ramsley walked in and smiled at Nikolai as he walked past him and into the Sergeant's office, on the other side of the briefing room.

The other officers walked in, and the last one to come through the door was Corporal Hardy. Nikolai stood up and reached for Hardy's hand and introduced himself. Hardy shook his hand and gave Nikolai a brief look-over and said, "Nice to meet you, rookie, we're gonna get through roll call and then have a chat." Nikolai nodded, and the two men sat back down.

Ramsley walked into the squad room, and it went from the sound of laughter and idle chit-chat to silence instantly. Ramsley barked, "Welcome to day shift, fucktards! Most of you know me, so I am gonna make this quick and to the point. I love this job, and I love to have fun doin' it. I am truly inspired by those who do self-initiated, proactive police work. That bein' said, folks, if you pick up an arrest or you're in the middle of something, you are expected to handle the call you are in rotation for. Don't, and I mean don't, dump your workload on someone else. Any of you pull that shit, its gonna cost you in your evaluation, and I will be detailed. Bottom line is this, we are a team, and I expect you each to look out for each other, get me?"

Everyone on the shift responded joyfully in their own way, either with an "Ooooh Rah" or a "Yes Sir."

Ramsley continued. "Next on the docket, we have our trainee assigned to FTO Hardy. Nikolai Drew, stand up son." Nikolai stood up and looked around the room; he was hard to miss, looking like a professional bodybuilder. Ramsley continued. "Our biggest challenge is drunks on the mall these days, gang, and that Gentleman Bank Robber is still out there makin' us look like idiots. The fucker hit us again yesterday, and the covering shift missed him. Keep your heads on a swivel out there, folks, and whoever gets this bastard will get a bottle of top shelf whiskey on me. You're all dismissed."

Hardy and Nikolai sat there for a few, and once the officers bailed out, Hardy began. "I have heard a great deal about you, kid, but I don't judge or make any assumptions. My plan is to assess you for a day or two, and after that, put you out on your own and ghost you, you know that term, yes?"

Nikolai said, "Yes sir, you will be around backing me up on all calls as you see fit, not necessarily at the onset of the call or self-initiated activity, but at some point."

Hardy smiled. "You get the drift. Set the car up, and let's get to it."

Nikolai went through his checklist, running the emergency equipment, checking the unit's oil level, and inventorying the trunk for missing equipment. There were no new dents, all the lights were working, and the trunk was fully stocked. Hardy walked out and took the passenger seat, and Nikolai pulled out of the station onto First Street, grabbed the radio microphone, pressed the button "2-Adam-27 is 10-8."

Dispatch parroted the report. "Roger 2-Adam-27 is 10-8." Nikolai headed east, turned onto Brand, and headed south toward the central business district. There was no radio traffic this morning, and Wednesdays were generally slow on day shift.

He looked over at his training officer and asked, "Do you mind if I throw out ideas, sir, you know, about what we can do to occupy our time between calls?"

Hardy grinned and replied, "By all means, kid, whaddaya got?"

Nikolai went on. "How about we walk a foot beat in the mall and grab a cup of coffee, I figure it will go a long way with the business owners if they see us walking around. Who knows, maybe we can pick up a 10-15 or two?"

Hardy smiled again and said, "The car is yours."

They arrived at the mall on the far East End, exited the unit, and Nikolai took out his handheld radio and reported to dispatch, "2-Adam-27 will be walking a footbeat on the mall." Dispatch again parroted the radio command.

They walked by the Bank of America building and into the bar on the north side of the street called Carter's Place. Hardy ordered two cups of coffee, and Nikolai took the opportunity to look around and even went into the men's restroom to see if there were any signs of drug activity or drunks milling about. It was quiet. Joel, the bartender, lived above the old bar in a one bedroom apartment. He was in his fifties and is well known as an OG with Pacoima Trece and joked with Hardy, "You still a lowly corporal, Hardy, this your newest rookie, Holmes? This kid looks like a pretty boy." Hardy gave the bartender a snide look and no response. Joel replied, "Coffee will be ready in a minute, just put on a fresh pot, you don't want that old shit that was in there!"

Hardy laughe., "Yup, just a lowly FTO mister, but honestly, I like the job, and this kid is a beast, no joke." Joel was always easy to deal with and would oftentimes give out some good info on what was happening gang wise if he trusted you but mostly if he felt like it would benefit the community.

The bartender poured the cups of coffee, and Nikolai put $3.00 on the bar, $1.50 for the coffee and the same for the tip. Nikolai put his hand out and thanked Joel for the coffee. He shook his hand and commented, "Anytime."

The two officers walked down San Fernando Road, and Hardy asked Nikolai, "So, we engage someone who is intoxicated walking down the mall right now, what would you do?"

Nikolai took a sip of his coffee and spit out a quick answer. "I'd observe him for a bit, then I'd say hello to him and see how his speech is, how he's standing, and if he's sober or intoxicated."

Hardy responded, "Okay, he's ripped, what next?"

"I'd cuff him, pat him down, sit him on the curb, and broadcast that we're Code 6 on one with our location, then run him for wants and warrants! Warrants or no warrants, he's going to jail for 647 f P.C., public drunkenness."

Hardy smirked and asked, "Okay, so you're good with doing the paperwork on this guy and spending the next couple of hours booking him and writing the arrest report?"

Nikolai snapped back quickly, "Hell yes I am, sir, no arrest is too big or too small."

Hardy patted him on the back and praised him. "That's the right answer, you see a need, cleaning up a potential situation, and by God you will get results, and you will get brownie points from the Chief for taking on a project no one else wants to do." They walked a total of two miles around the entire mall, greeted many people, and smiled at many of the small business owners who seemed to be in shock seeing patrol officers walking around the area.

As they made their way back down San Fernando Road toward their patrol car, Nikolai observed a male Hispanic in the doorway of a lunch spot that wasn't open yet. He wasn't sure he was seeing this with his own eyes, but yes, he noticed urine now running away from the deep alcove toward the street: the man was pissing on the door. He pointed the man out to Hardy, and the two men walked up to the man that they now realized was wearing no shoes, no shirt, and had his pants down to his knees and was wobbling quite noticeably. Nikolai cleared his throat. "Excuse me sir, you wanna put that away and turn around, please?"

The man raised immediately, turned around to his left, still relieving himself, and managed to urinate all over the pants of Training Officer Hardy. Hardy immediately spun the man back around to stop being soiled upon. "Nice job, Drew, for the love of fuck, pull your pants up, dirtbag. Jesus, you are a nasty thing!"

The drunk slurred his speech. "What are you doing in my house, that is no way to treat a taxpayer!"

Nikolai was snickering and doing his very best to hold back his laughter.

Hardy was still holding the drunk by the back of the neck and head against the window and sarcastically said, "Pull your fuckin pants up right God damned now!" Nikolai had put on rubber gloves he pulled out of his rear pocket and aided the inebriated man in pulling his pants up. The man barely got the top button attached, Nikolai finished the rest and was now fully disgusted by the smell coming from the man's body. Nikolai cuffed the man, and Hardy told him to go get the unit. Nikolai removed his handheld radio from the pouch on his Sam Browne utility belt and broadcast, "2-Adam 27, we're Code 6 on one in front of 912 San Fernando Road, Code 4 and 10-15 with one."

By the time he returned with the unit, there were people across the street watching what was going on. Nikolai exited the car and briskly approached Hardy and the drunk and helped escort the man to the back seat of the unit. The two men returned to the car, and Hardy grabbed the microphone as they pulled away from the curb. "27 control, be advised, we're enroute 10-19 with one 10-15!" Dispatch parroted the transmission. They arrived at the station, removed the man from the back seat of the car. Nikolai looked at his partner with a disgusted look on his face, noting that the dirty half-clad man had urinated all over the seat. As they walked into the jail, both men secured their weapons in the gun lockers. They made it to the holding cell where subjects await the booking process. Nikolai removed his cuffs and placed the drunk into the cell. The man lay down, and Nikolai secured the cell door. Hardy looked at him with a disgusted look on his face and half laughing.

"Alright, get his identification and have dispatch run him for warrants and get started on the report. I am going to get out of these clothes and shower up. I'll be back out quickly."

Nikolai went back into the booking cell. The jailer had already removed what little personal property the subject had in his possession and had it on the counter. Nikolai walked it up to dispatch, photocopied it, and handed the copy to the dispatcher. As he walked back toward the report room, Sergeant Ramsley walked in the back door of the station. "What did you bring in, kid?" After sniffing, he added to the comment. "Let me rephrase that, what nasty piece of shit did you bring in, damn it, rookie, you're supposed to only bring in clean suspects!"

Nikolai laughed, "Yeah, well that isn't the best part. He pissed all over my FTO and the inside of the unit, Sarge!"

Ramsley laughed out loud. "Oh, that must have gone over like a fart in church!" Ramsley walked into the locker room and Nikolai went about writing the arrest report.

Drunk in public reports were a one-page form that

identified the suspect, date, time, and location of arrest and a spot for a brief narrative. This was an infraction, meaning this is substantially less of an offense than a misdemeanor, so the report would be filed as would the booking record under an incident number along with fingerprints and a booking photo. The defendant in these types of cases simply receives a citation when released, upon becoming sober and fined at a later date. Dispatch informed Nikolai that the man in custody had no wants or warrants, which he added to the end of his report. Hardy came out of the locker room suited up and in a much better mood.

"What do you need me to do, kid?" he asked Nikolai.

The rookie handed him the file and said, "Just review it, sir and we can go ahead and go 10-8, I also already cleaned out the back seat of the patrol unit." Hardy looked over the package and turned it in, and the men walked back through the jail, and retrieved their weapons. They got back in their patrol car which already had the windows down. Nikolai grabbed the microphone and broadcast, "2-Adam-27, we're 10-8."

Dispatch parroted the response. "Roger 2-A-27, showing you 10-8."

The remainder of the shift was pretty quiet, and at one point, Hardy had Nikolai at the far south end of the patrol area they were assigned to. Hardy told Nikolai to drive as fast and safely in Code 2 as he could, no lights or siren,) to 385 N. Lazard Street.

Nikolai had already memorized most of the streets in all of the beats in the division, so this was an easy task. In less than three minutes, they arrived with no incident. Hardy expressed pleasure with Nikolai's performance. He had Nikolai write a couple of traffic tickets, one of which was to a driver with a suspended license, which resulted in them also impounding the driver's vehicle and sending him walking. End of the shift was at 4 p.m., so they arrived at the station at 3:45, cleared out the vehicle, and walked to the Sergeant's office. They all talked briefly, and Hardy told the Sergeant that he was going to have Nikolai work in a one man unit for the next several days so he could evaluate Nikolai from a distance. They were all in agreement, so Nikolai got out of his uniform and headed home. The traffic was brutal, taking nearly two hours to get to Riverside during rush hour. It was truly nerve racking.

CHAPTER
SIXTEEN

Nikolai working alone went very well on Thursday. He got out of his uniform and made his way back to the Detective Bureau to chat with Detective Bedo. The weekend was upon them, and Nikolai, in an attempt to be a productive part of the department, always liked knowing what he could do to assist others on their caseloads. Bedo looked up from his desk and smiled at the rookie. "What the fuck do you want, kid?" he asked, chuckling.

Nikolai smiled and said, "You know, Dad, the keys to the car and some cash for tonight's date!"

Bedo laughed, stood up, and escorted the rookie to the back door of the Detective Bureau. As they walked out, Bedo took a pack of cigarettes out of his shirt pocket, removed a smoke, and lit it.

Nikolai started the conversation. "The weekend is

comin' up. I know all you want for Christmas is this Gentleman Bank Robber, brother. I am on that all day, everyday, but is there something else you are lookin' for that I can keep an eye out for?"

Bedo took a drag from his cigarette and rubbed his hand through his hair. "Yeah, kid, I am lookin' for a burglar/hype/strong arm robbery suspect. His name is Joe Pimentel. I'll give you a recent booking photo of him; he's a piece of work. He is usually living on the street known to be hanging out at the Pacoima Wash under the bridge off San Fernando Road. Either one of these will get you a nice bottle of whatever you like!" They walked back inside the Detective Bureau where Bedo pulled a photo of Pimentel out of a file folder in his filing cabinet. Nikolai took it and with a big smile on his face told Bedo that he would have them both in custody by the end of the weekend!

Bedo patted the rookie on the back and said, "Go get 'em, kid."

The next morning Nikolai got in to work at 6:00 a.m. and drove around the city to see what was happening. He stopped at the Pacoima Wash bridges, one on Foothill Boulevard, one on 8th Street, and the last at San Fernando Road. There were about fifteen homeless sleeping under the bridges combined, and it was hard to tell if one of them was Pimentel, but, it was a good place to start.

He was already in his gym clothes, so he parked his El Camino and walked into the gym. He started stretching and warming up the joints. Today was chest day, so he was going to start with the decline press and get his first fifteen reps in, but, there was a guy already in the gym, one he had not seen before. The guy was roughly 5'7" and built like Franco Columbu, the famous body builder known for being friends with Arnold Schwarzenegger and writing a book called *Beginning Body Building*. Looking at the two men standing together, one would figure they looked like Arnold and Franco, but clearly Nikolai and Carbone were better looking, and Carbone seemed old enough to be Nikolai's father!

Nikolai put a forty-five and a twenty-five pound plate on each side of the forty-five pound bar on the decline bench and knocked out twenty reps to warm up. His gym-mate spoke up and asked him who he was, as he had never seen the rookie before.

Nikolai walked over and shook his hand and introduced himself. "Nikolai Drew, pleased to meet you."

Carbone smiled, "Well hi there, Nancy, I'm Pascuale Carbone. I'm a reserve. I've heard about you, scooby snack. You got in that shooting a couple months back, right?"

Nikolai grinned. "Yes, yes I did. Cundalini, is it? What the fuck is that, Spanish or Italiano? And its Nikolai, fucktard, not Nancy!" The two men went about their workouts. Carbone looked over and observed that Nikolai had 450 pounds on the flat bench and walked over to spot him. Carbone probably figured Nikolai was trying to impress him. But Nikolai not only lifted the weight with ease, he managed to do four very slow repetitions, and when he racked the weight, it was clear he had a few more in him. He paused and sat at the bench for a few moments, then got up to add some more weight. Now at 515 pounds, he sat at the bench and knocked out fifty reps of abdominals.

Carbone grinned at the rookie. "I meant Nancy as in Nancy Drew; don't get your panties in a bunch, as for the name, it's Carbone, and I'm a fucking Dago, ya rat bastard."

Carbone sat at the incline bench and knocked out twenty reps of 225 pounds, which is pretty impressive for a guy at fifty years old.

Nikolai laughed. "Well shit, man, I'm originally from Upstate New York, where you from, Jersey?"

Carbone laughed loudly. "Fuck you, I'm from Brooklyn, ya fuckin' putz!" As the workout went on, their dialogue grew even more colorful and insulting as the men bonded. It was clear they needed to work out together again; they were having a great time busting one another's balls.

Nikolai finished up the workout, showered, and suited up. After roll call, Nikolai rushed out to set up his vehicle. Training Officer Hardy walked out the back door and began setting up his own unit which was parked next to the rookie's. "What are you planning for today rookie?" Hardy asked.

Nikolai looked over at the two striper and said, "Well, sir, I thought I'd buy you a cup, then head out in search of knuckleheads who need a little guidance!"

Hardy laughed. "Alright, rook, I'll see you at 146 in about 10!"

Nikolai arrived at the 7-11, got two cups of coffee, and set up Hardy's the way he liked it, half coffee an half hot chocolate. The rookie paid for the drinks and walked outside to wait for the training officer. Hardy pulled up and put his hand out of the window of the unit, "Hand it over, kid, I gotta go get this shithead speeding up Hubbard like a bat outta hell." Nikolai handed Hardy the coffee and immediately got into his own unit and followed the training officer to find the speeding vehicle.

By the time they got back onto Hubbard, the white four-wheel drive Jeep was heading eastbound on Hubbard nearly at Glenoaks Boulevard. Hardy got about a quarter mile behind the speeding Jeep and turned on the overhead lights and hit the siren briefly to get the driver's attention. This is an old trick cops use to get someone to run rather than stop. If the offender is the slightest bit froggy, they will think that the officer is far enough behind that they can get away; such a bad idea, but the vehicle pursuit is fun for the officers involved.

In this case, the offender was not froggy and immediately pulled over. Hardy placed the middle of his unit at the left side bumper of the offender's vehicle and approached the driver's door. Nikolai approached the passenger side to act as cover and also put the traffic stop out over the radio letting dispatch know they were both on the traffic stop. The driver was a twenty-six-year-old busty brunette who lived at the corner of Hagar and 4th Street and was a paramedic known for being a badge bunny—a woman who loved dating policemen. Hardy asked her the customary questions and walked back to the passenger side of his vehicle to meet up with Nikolai.

Hardy knew who the woman was and asked Nikolai what he would do in this instance. Nikolai thought for a moment and responded, "Well sir, I'd probably let her off with a warning, for two reasons; first, because she lives in the city and second, because she stopped immediately."

Hardy smiled. "Oh, so it has nothing to do with her bra size? Alrighty then, Rookie, go let her off the hook, and don't make it look like you're staring at her tits while you do it!"

Nikolai approached the driver's door of the Jeep and smiled, "Ma'am, were going to let you off with a warning today, because you stopped immediately and because you live in town. Just please, please slow it down. This is a complaint area for traffic offenders, and you may not get this lucky next time."

As the rookie handed the license and registration for the vehicle back to the woman, she smiled, looked at his name tag, and said, "Well, Officer Drew, you must be new, I can tell because I never forget a name or a face! I live at Hagar and 4th Street. You should come by for a visit sometime; if I'm not working, I'm home!"

Nikolai tried to keep his eyes off the woman's chest, smiled, and said "I'll come by some time for sure, ma'am." As they got back in their respective patrol cars, Hardy informed dispatch they were back in service.

Nikolai headed back over to the Pacoima Wash Basin, looking for the homeless again, hoping to find Pimentel. Sadly, they had all woken up and were now meandering about like the walking dead either thieving, pan handling, or ticking off the locals. As he pulled away from San Fernando Road at the wash, dispatch broadcast, "Any unit in the area of the 900 block of San Fernando Road please advise."

Nikolai immediately responded, "2-L-27 is in the area!"

Dispatch responded, "Roger 27, respond to the area, there is a report of several 415 HBD's creating a disturbance, 4-5 male Hispanics NFD, unit to back identify."

Immediately another unit responded, "2-A-22 en route."

Nikolai arrived and immediately observed two

staggering men in their late 40s staggering while attempting to swing at one another. These were definitely the HBD's, or has been drinking. Their clothes were tattered and dirty, and one had no shirt on while three others swayed on their feet watching in earnest! Nikolai put out, "2-L-27, I'm Code 6 on 2 who appear to be severely HBD with three onlookers in the same condition." Code 6 meant aggressively contacting the subjects.

The backing unit also put out Code 6, and all officers engaged. The two men in the other unit were senior officers who let Nikolai act as the primary contact. Nikolai quickly put the aggressor in the fight in an arm bar, which disabled him and caused him to squeal in pain. Nikolai told the remaining four to sit down and put their hands on their knees. His voice was stern and direct and even caused the other two officers to get chills and want to obey the commands. All four did as they were told as Nikolai handcuffed and patted down the first subject. Nikolai asked the other officers, Cutler and Menso to please pat down the remaining subjects for weapons and assist with field interview cards. During the conversation with all five of the subjects, Nikolai noticed that all of them displayed subjective symptoms of alcohol intoxication, but two were different. He observed needle marks in the two men's arms. Upon further examination, he noticed that the two men's pulses were slow, at approximately 44 beats per minute.

Nikolai escorted each of the men individually into a shaded location while the other two officers covered the remaining detainees. Nikolai examined the men's pupils, and it was clear that these two were under the influence of heroin.

While Nikolai was performing the examination on the two addicts, he heard Cutler put out the name Joe Pimentel over the radio. He sat the two men down and could not believe how bad Pimentel looked. He was much worse looking than the photos he was given by Bedo. No wonder no one was able to find him lurking about. He looked half dead! He removed his handheld radio from its case and put in a call to Detective Bedo. "2-L27 to 13 David," he called out.

Bedo quickly responded, "13 David go!"

Nikolai told him to switch to frequency 2. Bedo switched and called out, "13 David on 2, go ahead, kid."

Nikolai grinned as he responded, "I just found Pimentel, and I'll have him in the station in about five."

Bedo was clearly ecstatic as he replied, "Copy 27, good job, see you in five."

Nikolai had enough, they were all going in for public drunkenness at the very least. They would figure out the warrant situation during booking. Not only was he clearing up the drunks on the mall for the Chief, he was helping Bedo and doing it all where the public could see. Nikolai directed the other two officers to assist him cuffing the five men and help transport them to the police station for booking. Three were cuffed and loaded into one car and two in Nikolai's unit. As he entered his vehicle, he grabbed the microphone on the dash and put out, "2-L-27 to control, show this unit and A-22 en route 10-19 with five 10-15's."

Moments later, both units arrived at the police station. They were met by Detective Bedo, who assisted them in escorting the five men into the booking cells. The jailer began patting them down and determining who was who and what the charges would be for each. Bedo on the other hand discreetly told the jailer to go about booking Pimentel like the others, but to also add the charge of 459 and 211 of the penal code but not to share that information with Pimentel or the others. He wanted time to interview him first.

Cutler and Menso asked Nikolai if he needed anything else. He told them no, he would handle it. Before Nikolai retreated to the report room, he walked back into the booking area and asked the jailer to be sure to put Cutler's and Menso's names with his own in the arrest log book.

He sat at the report writing counter and began putting together the drunk in public arrest reports for three of the suspects. Bedo walked in and gave him a high five.

Nikolai was extremely pleased with himself and

asked, "Hey, brother, how do you want me to write up the arrest on Pimentel?"

Bedo told him "Simply write the observation arrest for drunk in public and then note that you notified me that you had him in custody and brought him in. I will be writing my own report, and I'm adding burglary and robbery to the charges as well, and my report will cross reference yours, you will get the stat. Great job, that guy looks like hell. No wonder no one has picked him up; he's a shell of the man we were looking for!"

Hardy pulled into the station and walked into the report room about thirty minutes after Nikolai arrived at the station. Nikolai was just finishing up the arrest reports and getting ready to book the two heroin addicts' urine specimens into evidence. The two men walked down the hallway to the evidence room, and as Nikolai filled out the evidence log, pulled the carbon copy off and slid it into the locker with the specimens, Hardy pat him on the back and praised him for a great job, "You did some great work out there, I watched most of the contact, pat down and arrest. Let me take a look at the paperwork before we head out."

They walked down the hall and into the Sergeant's office, and Nikolai took the report folder from the desk, placed the evidence paperwork in the file, and handed it to Hardy. The Field Training Officer read it all pretty quickly. After all, it was a short report, but the content was brief and well put. "Nice report writing kid, I also checked the heroin addicts' vitals before coming up, and I concur with your findings. You've done more in the first four hours of the day than most do in a week, kid. Keep this up, and you'll have every lazy patrolman pissed at you for life," Hardy said, half laughing. As the two men walked out of the station to their patrol cars, Hardy asked Nikolai if he wanted to grab lunch. Nikolai thought for a moment then said he was going to grab something on the fly. He had some things he wanted to check out. Nikolai grabbed the microphone as he backed out of the jail parking lot and put himself 10-8, back in service.

SEVENTEEN

Nikolai pulled out of the back of the station and had to hit the brakes hard as a civilian car was pulling in at high speed. That car came to a screeching stop, nearly colliding head on with the police cruiser. Nikolai's heart was racing, adrenaline flowing through him, and he felt the anger, then looked at the driver of the other vehicle. It was Sully; his eyes were wide open, both hands on the wheel, and he looked frantic. Nikolai backed up, and Sully pulled up alongside him. "I am so sorry, Drew, damn that was close!"

Nikolai smiled and let it pass, and as Sully drove past, Nikolai saw him nose into a parking space, get out, and look pensively at Nikolai as he pulled out onto First Street. There was a lot of squabble on the scanner, units in North Hollywood attempting to find a robbery suspect fleeing on foot wearing a dark blue jumpsuit, a black ski mask, black leather gloves, and combat boots.

Nikolai stopped his patrol car, and all of it started coming together. Sully looking sheet-white, eyes bulging, all the times he'd run into him coming into the station and every goddamn time, it was right after the Gentleman Bank Robber had hit. He shut the car off, parked at the curb, and walked back to the rear parking area of the police station where Sully had parked his car. Nikolai was playing this back in his head. *Am I over thinking this? Am I fucking crazy? Who the fuck is gonna believe me? I gotta have physical evidence*, he thought to himself as he made his way to Sully's car, carefully. The driver's side door was ajar, and the seat belt sticking out between the door jam. He looked in the vehicle, and behind the driver's seat on the floor was a ski mask like reported in so many of the robberies. *But is this enough?* he thought. He opened the passenger door of the silver 1984 Buick Le Sabre, looking around carefully, then opened the glove box and hit the trunk release button. He quickly moved to the back of the car which was fully exposed to anyone walking out of the station, or pulling into the parking lot, and found a dark blue jumpsuit, boots, and leather gloves. Beneath all that was a gym bag. He quickly looked in it and saw what looked like several thousand dollars in cash. He returned everything as he found it.

Nikolai quickly returned to his patrol unit, started

it up and drove to the detective side of the building, parked his car, walked to the detective door and knocked loudly. Bedo answered the door, walked outside, and removed a cigarette from the pack in his shirt. As he lit it, he asked Nikolai what was up.

Nikolai was feeling wild, his pupils were dilated, and he was thinking so many things in his head.

"Talk to me kid, you look like you're gonna have a stroke," Bedo said as he took the cigarette from his mouth.

Nikolai gave it a moment, then spoke. "Look, you're not gonna fuckin' believe this, but I have the Gentleman Bank Robber, and you are not gonna believe who it is!"

Bedo leaned against his detective unit, crossed his arms, and spoke. "You know who the Gentleman Bank Robber is, and I am not gonna believe it? Well fuck me, kid, spill, who is it and how do you know?"

Nikolai looked at him and told him about all the coincidences and peculiar instances with Reserve Officer Sully. He then told him about how Sully nearly hit him head on and had to skid to a stop to avoid the collision a little bit ago and told him that he saw the ski mask on the floorboard of Sully's car behind the driver's seat.

Detective Bedo was mulling the next move over and over in his head. "Follow me. We need to chat with the lieutenant. This is an interesting one, kid." They walked into the police station and shut the lieutenant's office door behind them. Lieutenant Quinton McHale was a 5'7", 155 pound, sixty-two-year-old triathlete who had served ten years in the United States Marine Corps. He was known for being an asskicker and finding the means to put a case to bed based on a hunch over his thirty-five-year career in law enforcement. Bedo set the table and gave him all the information that was given him by Nikolai.

The lieutenant sat back in his chair and rested his chin on his left hand as he tapped his right hand on the butt of his 4" stainless steel Colt Python revolver that rested on his hip, simultaneously looking at Nikolai skeptically. "Drew, I have heard good shit about you. You know what this means. If we do what needs to be done to get this guy in custody, and it's a shit show right? It means that you, me, and Bedo go down as fucktards, and this guy Sully owns this department financially, you get that right?"

Nikolai nodded. "I do, sir, I am aching inside over this, but the mask is there, and I am willing to bet that the money and the outfit are in his trunk or in his locker in the station!" Nikolai didn't want to reveal that he had already been in the trunk of the car; he wanted the obvious evidence to tell the story.

Lieutenant McHale looked at the two men before him intently, then told Bedo, "Write the warrant and get across the street and get it signed off by a judge. We need this done like now before Sully bails out."

Nikolai interjected, "Sir, if I am right, every time

he comes in after pulling off a robbery, he suits up and goes 10-8. He must be listening to the scanner the entire time to figure out what we know."

Lieutenant McHale barked again, "Bedo, get that shit done, get it signed, and get back here ASAP. When we get it, let's me, you, and the kid execute the warrant together, quietly. I'd like to do this in a way that no one knows what's up, so if we're wrong, we can put a cork in it without burning Sully or ourselves. Move, move, move. Drew, stick around. Be available in the station for when Bedo returns. If you get a call, go about your business; if we have to do this alone, we will."

Bedo ran to his desk and wrote up the warrant in less than fifteen minutes then went over to a judge he trusted. Fortunately Judge Tynan was in his office sitting at his desk in a shirt and tie and wearing sweatpants and tennis shoes, a practice often used by judges.

"Judge, do you have a moment, sir?" Bedo asked.

The judge smiled and replied, "Always for you, young man. What is the urgency in your voice that I detect?" Bedo laid out the reason for the warrant as the judge read it.

The judge smiled. "Well damn, if this kid is right, he has one hell of a keen sense to him. How do you intend to protect him if this goes down. You know how cops feel about burning cops?"

Bedo ran his hand through his hair. "I have to tell

you, Judge, this has been puzzling me since it was brought to my attention. We will cross that bridge when we burn it, I suppose!" The judge signed the warrant and bid Detective Bedo good luck. Bedo practically ran back to the police station. He walked into the Detective Office, waved the warrant at Lieutenant McHale, and they together walked down the hall toward the back of the station where Sully's car was parked.

As they exited the back door, Nikolai was standing watch and told the two men that Sully was still in the field and had been since this all started just over an hour ago. The men approached the car, looking around to make certain that no one was watching. Bedo opened the unlocked driver's door and observed the ski mask just as described by Nikolai. He leaned over the glove box and opened it, hoping to find a trunk release, otherwise, they'd have to break in, or call Sully in to have him open it. Luckily, the trunk had an electronic release. He hit the button and exited the vehicle. As he approached Lieutenant McHale and Nikolai, they together pulled the jumpsuit aside and found the gloves, boots and a gym bag. Bedo unzipped the bag, and as he opened it, the lieutenant exclaimed, "Well, fuck me, good goin', Drew. This is gonna be good and bad; God damn it!"

Nikolai, distressed, replied, "I know L.T., it never goes over well when a cop outs another, but this is a big one. I'll take the hit, whatever it means."

Bedo shook his head. "You need to take a real soft approach to this, kid. You're still on probation for a few more months. You need to never act proud, rather solemn about what this is going to turn into." Nikolai agreed, and they began the process of collecting evidence and taking pictures. Once the evidence was gathered and documented, Bedo took it all into the evidence room and secured it, then had the watch Sergeant's office and told him what they had and asked him to call Officer Sully in, nonchalantly. Bedo walked out of the office and got Lieutenant McHale to stand inside the back door of the station where Sully would be walking in. Nikolai walked up to the two men and asked what they wanted him to do. Bedo told him, "You get outta here, go 10-8, and go about your business. This is in our lap now."

Nikolai walked out and pulled out of the station and headed to the 7-11 located at 146 Hubbard. He had butterflies in his stomach as the severity of all this was not setting in. In his head, he knew this was the right thing to do and recognized that he didn't force Sully to be a robber. In his head, he knew he would face scrutiny. He just needed to go about his duties and never let it get to him.

Ten minutes went by, and Sully walked into the back door of the station and was greeted by the Lieutenant and Detective Bedo. Bedo quickly removed Sully's side arm from its holster and put it in the back of his trousers and handcuffed him without incident.

Sully was furious. "What in the hell are you guys doing?"

Bedo asked him "Are you carrying a knife or backup gun?"

Sully responded, "Yes, knife in my left front pocket, no other guns. What the fuck is going on Bedo?"

Bedo patted him down, retrieved the knife and ran his hands over his pockets and down his pant legs and found a .38 snub nosed revolver on an ankle holster on Sully's left ankle. Bedo removed the weapon, placed it in his rear pocket, and the two men quietly moved the officer into an interview room in the jail, walking past the jailer who had a shocked look on his face.

Lieutenant McHale stopped briefly and told the jailer, "Not a word to anyone on this, you understand, mister?"

The jailer snapped to attention and said, "Yes sir, not a word."

In the interview room, Bedo removed Sully's utility belt, handed it to the lieutenant, and had him sit down. Bedo recited to Sully, "Officer Sully, you are under arrest for multiple robberies. You have the right to remain silent. Anything you say may be used against you in a court of law. You have the right to an attorney. If you cannot afford an attorney, one will be appointed for you before questioning. Do you understand each of these rights I have read to you?"

Sully's face went from surprise and anger to a saddened look of grief as he slumped into his chair. "Yes, I understand my rights. Fuck, how did you catch me?"

Bedo sat down and put his hand together in front of him. "I'll tell you what I know, but I need you to tell me what you know first."

Sully bit his lip, he sat up straight. "Look man, a few years ago, my wife filed for divorce. I hit a bank in Hollywood and got out with about twenty thousand. It helped me pay the attorney's fees and get her off my back, for the moment. I immediately drove to the station, suited up, and went 10-8, so I could hear what was going on over the scanner. It got worse, she wanted more and more money, the blood sucking vampire, so I did another. It was easy, quick in, quick out, and I never used or carried a gun."

Bedo was recording this all on video. "How many banks have you hit and how long have you been doing this?"

Sully thought for a moment then replied, "I have hit twenty-eight over the last three years, Bedo. From here to Ventura County."

Bedo was in disbelief of how easy this was, but then again, the turmoil felt by a cop perpetrating this kind of thing had to weigh on him. This had to be like a purging. Bedo continued questioning. "How much do you think you have gotten away with up to this point?"

Sully immediately responded, "One million three hundred and fifty thousand, not counting today's take, did you find that?"

Bedo nodded, and told him they had collected $28,000.00 in the gym bag in his trunk.

Sully was bewildered. "How did you put it together, Bedo? No one ever saw me, and I never left prints. No one ever suspected a thing, and the last I heard, there were no leads, so what the hell, where did I slip up?"

Bedo told him, "An officer has seen you come into the station several times after the robberies, and today, you nearly ran into him. He came back after you parked to check on you and found your driver's door ajar.

"As he approached the car, he saw the ski mask on the floor in the back seat and immediately came to see me. I wrote up a warrant, got it signed, and the rest is history. Where is the rest of the money you took?"

Sully shook his head. "Fucking Nikolai Drew, that rookie piece of shit! I knew it when he looked at me as I drove by him after I almost hit him, but honestly, I never thought he'd do any digging. I have about $800,000.00 in the master bedroom at my house. It's in a safe. I'll give you the combo. There are a bunch of guns too, Bedo, all legal."

There was a long pause as the two men sat across from one another. Sully took a deep breath and said with a solemn look on his face, "Ya know, I am almost relieved. This shit was getting out of hand."

Bedo stood up and walked the officer to booking. As he handed Sully off to the jailer, he said, "Do me a favor, get the uniform shirt, gun leather, and his Police ID, and bring it to my office when you have him put away, please."

Bedo and the Lieutenant now had the arduous task of going to the Chief's office to report what had happened. Being four p.m. they stood a chance of not finding him around. Together they approached the Chief's secretary's desk and asked if he was in. She informed the men that he was indeed and to walk right in, he wasn't busy. As they entered the Chief's office, he stood up, shook their hands, and said, "To what do I owe the pleasure, gentlemen."

Lieutenant McHale began, "Well Chief, this is by no means a social call."

Chief Belknap walked around the desk and motioned for the men to sit in his leather couches that were at the front of his desk. They all sat down, and Chief Belknap put his hands on his knees. "Please don't tell me we have another injured officer!"

Bedo piped in "No sir, but it's almost as bad. We caught the Gentleman Bank Robber today."

Belknap smiled and said, "Well hell, I thought you

were gonna give me bad news. That's fantastic, who made the collar and how?"

Bedo went through all of the events of the arrest and the Chief's face went from pleased to disgust rather quickly. He sat there for a moment, pensive. After a few moments he perked up and said, "Well, that Nikolai Drew is one hell of a cop isn't he. I mean hell, from nearly getting himself killed to now taking down the Gentleman Bank Robber. Hell, I oughta promote the bastard. There is going to be some backlash. Cops like Sully, and you know as well as I do that they absolutely DO NOT like when officers turn on other officers. Either of you have any thoughts on this? I do, but I'd like to hear your take on the matter."

Lieutenant McHale began, "Yeah, Chief, we have a full confession, we need not disclose how we came up with any of this and need not burn Nikolai. The only people who know that Nikolai had anything to do with this are the three of us and him of course. The media is going to have a field day burning us in effigy for a cop performing the robberies and at the same time, patting us on the back for catching it ourselves. The question is will the kid keep his mouth shut?"

Chief Belknap smiled. "He's a legacy cop. He knows what to say and what not to, but I will have a chat with him myself before I head home, I like the plan.

"Bedo, do me a favor when you get done with the

paperwork on this mess and write something up about the kid so I can put an atta-boy in his file will you please?" The three men stood up, shook hands, and Bedo assured the Chief he would have him something in writing soon.

Chief Belknap walked to the dispatch center and asked them to have Officer Drew respond to the station, but not to divulge anything further. The dispatcher clicked the mic. "2-L-27, respond 10-19 for one please." This would seem like the dispatcher needed a restroom break. Nikolai responded "2-L-27, roger, en route."

Within moments Nikolai arrived at the station and approached the main hall to head to the dispatch center. Chief Belknap was poised in a hallway adjacent to the dispatch and called to Nikolai quietly, "Come with me for a moment son, will you."

Nikolai got that sick feeling in his stomach again. It was like heading to the principal's office. The Chief opened the back door to the office. They walked past the Chief's private bathroom, and they sat in the Chief's leather couch area at the front of his desk. Chief Belknap smiled at the rookie. "Well, son, you have had another interesting day! Your career here is going to be full of these challenges, I can tell already."

Nikolai nodded. "Are you disappointed in me, Chief?"

Belknap smiled and laughed. "Quite the contrary

son, I am very proud of you. You have handled something that many would have never wanted to address, a crooked cop." The Chief looked at Nikolai intently and continued. "You not only recognized a critical issue, but you brought it to the people who would be able to address it and stop this from becoming a colossal cluster fuck. Do you realize that this could have turned into a shootout with innocent civilians and other officers hurt? You have nothing to be ashamed of, but, I need you to do something for you and the department, okay?"

Nikolai responded, "Of course, Chief, anything."

Belknap patted him on the shoulder. "Good son, good, I want you to never speak of this to anyone. If anyone asks you about it outside Bedo, Lieutenant McHale, or myself, shrug it off like you don't know what they are talking about. Sully made a full confession. This will likely never go to trial but rather be settled with a plea bargain. The press will get a simple statement from me about the arrest and how we handled it in house, never bringing your name into it. The reality is that the Thin Blue Line never needs to know that an officer had anything to do with this. Can you do that, son?"

Nikolai was relieved. "Chief, this was my biggest concern, I didn't know how I was going to handle having to deal with some of the guys I work with, especially the reserves. Thank you!"

Chief Belknap stood, shook Nikolai's hand and

said, "You're a little over two months away from completing your probation. I want nothing to get in the way of that. Now, get back to work, that's five arrests for the day, all I can say is damn good job, son, you do the department and your entire bloodline of lawmen proud." Nikolai headed down the hall toward the back door of the station where his patrol unit was parked. His heart was no longer heavy, and his mind was clear.

As he approached the jail, he peeked in the door, and there was Sully, standing in the corner of the booking cell. Nikolai pondered for a moment then walked in and stared at the Reserve Police Officer.

Nikolai could see the disgust on Sully's face. He leaned over the booking counter and said in a low but deep and clear voice, "We have a hard enough time doing this job without people like you shittin' all over the badge and the public's trust! You didn't just hurt yourself today, dickhead, you shit all over all of us, all of us!" He slammed his hand against the steel screen in disgust then walked out of the jail. He walked out the back door of the station, entered the driver's door of his black and white, grabbed the microphone, pressed the call button and said with vigor, "2-L-27, I'm 10-8!"

THE END

APPENDIX

Law Enforcement Radio 10 Code
For Los Angeles County

10-0: Caution

10-1: Reception Poor

10-2: Reception Good

10-3: Stop Transmitting

10-4: Message Received, Understood

10-5: Repay Message

10-6: Change Channel

10-7: Responding

10-8: In Service

10-9: Repeat Message

10-10: Negative

10-11: Identify Frequency

10-12: Visitor(s) Present

10-13: Weather and Road Advice

10-14: Citizen w/ Suspect

10-15: Prisoner In Custody

10-16: Pick Up Prisoner

10-17: Request For Gasoline

10-18: Equipment Exchange

10-19: Return(ing) To Station

10-20: Location

10-21: Telephone

10-21A: Advise Home I Will Return At:

10-22: Disregard Last Assignment

10-23: Stand By

10-24: Request Car-To-Car Transmit

10-25: Do You Have Contact With:

10-26: Clear

10-27: D.D.L Report

10-28: Registration Request

10-29: Check For Wants

10-29F: Subject Wanted / Felony

10-29H: Hazard Potential From Subject

10-29M: Subject Wanted / Misdemeanor

10-29V: Vehicle Wanted

10-30: Doesn't Conform To Regulations

10-32: Drowning

10-33: Alarm Sounding, Audible

10-34: Assist At Office

10-35: Time Check

10-36: Confidential Information

10-37: Identify Operator

10-39: Can () Come To The Radio?

10-40: Is () Available For Phone Call?

10-42: Check The Welfare Of/At:

10-43: Call A Doctor

10-45: Condition Of Patient

10-45A: Good

10-45B: Serious

10-45C: Critical

10-45D: Dead

10-49: Proceed To:

10-50: Under Influence Of Drugs

10-51: Drunk

10-52: Resuscitator -53: Man Down

10-54: Possible Dead Body

10-55: Coroner Case

10-56: Suicide

10-56A: Suicide Attempt

10-57: Missing Person

10-59: Security Check

10-60: Lock-Out

10-61: Miscellaneous Public Service

10-62: Meet A Citizen

10-62A: Take A Report From A Citizen

10-62B: Civilian Standby

10-63: Prepare To Copy

10-64: Found Property

10-66: Suspicious Person

10-67: Person Calling For Help

10-68: Telephone For Police

10-70: Prowler

10-71: Shooting

10-72: Gun Involved

10-73: How Do You Receive?

10-79: Bomb Threat

10-80: Explosion

10-86: Any Radio Traffic?

10-88: Assume Post

10-91: Animal

10-91A: Animal Stray

10-91B: Animal Noisy

10-91C: Animal Injured

10-91D: Animal Dead

10-91E: Animal Bite

10-91G: Animal Pickup

10-91J: Animal Pickup Collect

10-91L: Animal Leash Law Violation

10-91V: Animal Vicious

10-95: Need Id Tech Unit

10-97: Arrived At Scene

10-98: Available To Assign

www.ingramcontent.com/pod-product-compliance
Lightning Source LLC
Chambersburg PA
CBHW070107030426
42335CB00016B/2053